THE
ANGEL
NUMBERS
BOOK

How to Understand the
Messages Your Spirit Guides
Are Sending You

MYSTIC MICHAELA

ADAMS MEDIA

NEW YORK   LONDON   TORONTO   SYDNEY   NEW DELHI

Adams Media
An Imprint of Simon & Schuster, Inc.
100 Technology Center Drive
Stoughton, Massachusetts 02072

First Adams Media hardcover edition November 2021

ADAMS MEDIA and colophon are trademarks of Simon & Schuster.

For information about special discounts for bulk purchases, please contact Simon & Schuster Special Sales at 1-866-506-1949 or business@simonandschuster.com.

The Simon & Schuster Speakers Bureau can bring authors to your live event. For more information or to book an event contact the Simon & Schuster Speakers Bureau at 1-866-248-3049 or visit our website at www.simonspeakers.com.

Interior design by Michelle Kelly
Images © 123RF/Nikki Zalewski

Manufactured in the United States of America

4 2023

ISBN 978-1-5072-1735-1

DEDICATION

For Scott, Breanna, and Abigail

CONTENTS

INTRODUCTION

Have you ever noticed yourself waking up at exactly the same time every night? Or find yourself stuck on a certain page number of a book? What about seeing those very numbers repeated on signs and license plates while you travel? Numbers fill your world, from your bank account and the schedule of your day to important dates and directions for caring for your health. Numbers are helpful, universal—and, most importantly, meaningful. That's why they make such a wonderful medium for your angel guides to send you messages.

What is an angel guide? In simple terms, an angel guide is a divine vibration tasked with helping you grow and achieve your life goals. Your angel guides exist to see you flourish! Numbers repeated throughout your day are one major way that they communicate guidance, warnings, and praise to let you know whether the path you are on is right for you. That time you wake up every night? That book page number you get stuck on? Those repeated numbers on signs and license plates? There are words of wisdom from your angel guides hidden within all of those numbers!

The Angel Numbers Book will help you decipher these messages. Here you'll receive the tools you need to understand the meaning of each number and number pattern sent by your angel guides. You'll also find space to record and reflect on the numbers you see, cultivating meanings that are personal to you and your experiences.

In Part 1, you'll explore what angel numbers are, how individual angel numbers and sequences hold specific meanings, and how to interpret the general ideas of angel numbers on your own. In Part 2, you'll discover a comprehensive codex of angel number sequences and their meanings, and specific steps you can implement if you receive that sequence. And in Part 3, you'll use a personalized log to record your angel number sightings and decode them. Through this log, you can notice the patterns that are unique to you, which will help you become more connected to your angel guides.

Through this book, you'll learn to turn your attention toward the communications of your angel guides, strengthen your understanding of the messages they are sending, and become tuned in whenever they're trying to speak to you. When you take the time to process their messages, you can use the knowledge of your angel guides to manifest your aspirations. It's time to use angel numbers to unlock your potential and light the way to a more satisfying, meaningful life!

Part 1

AN INTRODUCTION TO ANGEL NUMBERS

Seeing numbers in your daily life is just the start of your journey into deciphering them. You will begin to understand not only whom these messages are coming from, but also how to create a unique relationship with the angel guides sending them. This part of the book will dive into more detail about what angel numbers are, how to decipher their messages, and what to do with those messages. You will uncover how individual angel numbers and sequences hold specific meanings and learn to interpret the general idea of your angel number sightings on your own. The most powerful skill this part will teach you is the ability to construct your own meaning so that when you see numbers, you also see yourself within them! There is also instruction into how to further your communication by using the numbers from your angel guides to strengthen your link to the universe around you.

WHAT ARE ANGEL NUMBERS?

There seems to be a pattern among us. For centuries in human history, across different cultures and geographical locations, humans have asked the same question: "Why am I here?" We all want answers as to what our main purpose is in life—to what would make us feel happy and fulfilled and bigger than ourselves. Angel numbers are high-frequency messages that can help you answer that question for yourself. Why numbers specifically? Numbers occur in every place both on and beyond earth. Their patterns are found in everything that surrounds you, governing the planet's movements, the weather, sound, light, and even your own DNA. Number patterns exist in the most infinite reaches of your imagination and inward to the microcosm of your being. Because they are universal, they are the perfect medium for sending messages.

WHO IS SENDING THESE MESSAGES?

The high-vibrational beings who are the embodiment of such universal emotions as unconditional love, compassion, and forgiveness are called angels. They serve the divine, or the source of all life and energy on this planet, and also protect and guide you through your life. You have come here into this earth with a "soul contract," a predetermined checklist of objectives and lessons your higher self has deemed essential for this lifetime. (Your higher self is your soul's consciousness: the part of you that transcends your physical body. It is your eternal spirit.) Angel guides who have been assigned to you consistently remind you of the goals of your soul contract through angel numbers. And when you are progressing in your life, touching upon critical times and ascending into personal growth, the frequency at which your angels send numbers amps up!

Your life has incredible meaning. You have come here to help others, contribute to the world, and grow and learn as an individual. Your angels will send you messages to either remind you to get back on track or reevaluate a situation, or simply as a pat on the back for work well done. Your angels want you to feel supported in your journey on this earth, because you are. Their messages remind your higher self to stay focused and empowered along the way.

Angels are not the only ones who send numbers, however. Your loved ones who have passed on can also send you numbers. Oftentimes those who have passed use the language of numbers to get your attention, to let you know they are near you, offering their love and support, or to alert you to a special time or event that was important to them. These types of numbers are often linked to numbers in the sender's life, such as a birthday, anniversary, or date of passing.

WHERE CAN I SEE THESE NUMBERS?

Your angels are creative with the ways they deliver your number messages, and they use repetition as a key signal to pay attention. When you begin to focus more carefully on them, the numbers in your daily life really begin to pop! You will see repetitive numbers on paperwork, hear them being spoken by others, and even notice them as actual symbolic representations of a number itself, such as a configuration of birds sitting on your car, or the shape you find the snow has melted on a path you happen to be walking on. They will show up in innocuous places such as unread messages in your email, mysterious phone numbers calling you, and even sometimes in songs on your playlist!

Angel numbers are delivered in a myriad of ways. But a common thread binds them all: curiosity. When you open your mind up to possibility, your angels' messages will enter. As you will learn later, where, how, and when you see angel numbers all are integral in helping you decode their meaning. But seeing them at all will be a result of your being open to do so!

SYNCHRONICITY VERSUS COINCIDENCE

Your angels will send you a number more than once or twice. It will be a repeating pattern meant to capture your attention! Taking careful note of patterns and their frequency is the key to understanding whether you are seeing a true angel number or a mere coincidence. A number that stands out to you is interesting, but that same number finding you repeatedly throughout the day, week, or month signifies a specific message—what is known as synchronicity. Synchronicity is the moment when spiritual incidents are interconnected, yet not logically so. When coincidence becomes an unreasonable explanation, synchronicity is at play. And this is where your angel guides work their wonders! Angels will use the phenomenon of synchronicity to speak to you.

UNDERSTANDING THE NUMBERS

Angels communicate on a high-vibrational frequency fueled by love, emotion, and the unseen yet powerful pushes and pulls in the world around us. Because numbers occur in our natural world, they, too, have high-vibrational energy—a pull that brings forth ideas, reminders, and messages for moving forward.

Numbers have long been a source of interest and intrigue. Many religions, cultures, and alternative and new age theories incorporate numeric symbolism and look for insight in the energetic pull of certain numbers. Truly, people have pondered the universal code that numbers offer for centuries. This has developed over time into what is known as numerology, or the study of the meaning of numbers. Numerology is where the ideas and lessons of each angel number has been derived from. Each number in numerology has foundational themes that guide our understanding and play into how we decipher our own angel numbers.

CARDINAL NUMBERS 0–9

The cardinal numbers 0–9 are the single digits upon which angel number sequences are built. Because it's easier to notice numbers when they come in sequences, you will rarely see cardinal numbers standing alone in a message. Your angels rely on heavy repetition and sequencing to get your attention!

While each number holds a unique meaning, the interpretations of each number will vary because it must be paired within the context of your life and what you're going through presently. For example, the cardinal number 9 traditionally signifies an ending of some sort—a movement from one chapter to the next. Seeing this number while you are dealing with the passing of a loved one could mean you are being supported by your angels. Meanwhile, seeing it when you are contemplating leaving a very stressful job could indicate a divine nudge to get your resume out there sooner rather than later. Your meaning for each number may also vary because of your relationship with your angels, and even more so as you develop and strengthen that communication. For instance, if you see the number 9 often throughout life in many different contexts, it could be a personal "hello" from your angel guides. As you will explore in more detail later in this part, the placement of each number in a sequence is also important to make note of.

THREE- AND FOUR-DIGIT SAME-NUMBER SEQUENCES

Angels love to make a splash with their numeric messages, and nothing does this quite like a sequence of three or four repeated numbers. When you spot a sequence of 111, for example, it means to stop where you are right now. The cardinal number 1 signifies creation in your life in some manner. Perhaps you are in the midst of an important project, relationship, or reboot of your attitude. The number 1 signifies that *you* are the creator of your universe. Therefore, seeing it repeated is a direct message that right now the universe is taking a "screenshot" of your life and is about to replicate it for the future. Your angels want you to get on track with aligning your thoughts with your life goals. (See the meanings for each triple digit number in Part 2.) If you start seeing the four-digit sequence 1111, it means the same thing—but with a bit more urgency. When you see a fourth digit in a same-number sequence, think of it as an exclamation mark that your angels are sending you to move on this message fast!

SPIRIT SEQUENCES

Spirit sequences are special sets of numbers that tend to pose as predetermined messages from your angels. Seeing 711, for example, is a call to persistence. The cardinal number 7 is a reminder to not let fear control your choices moving forward, and the master number 11 conveys that you are undergoing a creative awakening and are being called to pay attention to it. So the number 711 signifies that your angels are calling you to honor your growth by reaping the rewards you've earned through your hard work. It usually denotes a leveling up in life due to the focused efforts you've undergone on a project or situation.

A "stepping stone" number is a signal from your angels to keep the faith. When you see this number, your angels are acknowledging that you are in the middle of a long project or journey, but that it will all be worth it in the end. While the primary stepping stone number is 123, any sequence of inclining digits that you see repeatedly can be a stepping stone number if it fits into a situation you are facing. Seeing a stepping stone number backward, the primary example being 321, is a nudge to eliminate forces that can move against your progress. For example, seeing 321 when deciding whether to eat fast food or cook at home tonight may be a message from your angels to stay on course for your health. Seeing 321 while in the midst of a stressful group project at work may ask you to reconsider who you have chosen to be on your team.

Spirit sequences tend to be uniquely doled out by your angels as you strengthen your bond. The more you talk to them, the more they creatively display these more detailed sequences as little reminders that they are present and supportive.

INTERPRETING YOUR ANGEL NUMBERS

Your angels want to talk to you, but it's up to you to decipher how the meanings of the numbers you receive fit into your unique life experience. So how do you do that? The following are a few simple guidelines for interpreting the messages you're receiving from your guides.

BREAK IT DOWN

When considering the meaning of an angel number, one way to interpret is by breaking it down. The cardinal numbers in a message are your keys to unlock its meaning. Here, order is imperative!

1. The first digit in the sequence will point to the situation(s) that led you to this particular moment. This digit often provides the "tone" of the entire sequence. For example, numbers beginning with 8 will have to do with an abundance mindset in some way, while numbers beginning with 3 will ask you to look at the way you are balancing priorities.

2. The central digit gives you the core message of the entire sequence. For example, a central number 2 reflects a need to increase gratitude, while a central number 5 points to major changes on the horizon with your current reality. In two-digit sequences, you will look at the second digit. Often with two-digit sequences, a third, final digit will be made clear to you later. When looking at a four-digit number, the two numbers in the middle will together make up the central digit. Identify the meaning of each number and interpret how they can fit together into one larger core meaning.

3. The last digit will point to your likely future outcome. For example, a final digit 9 will alert you to an impending ending of a chapter in your life, while a final digit 1 points to coming opportunities for manifesting your best life.

There is an exception, however. Master numbers, or numbers that repeat, such as 11, 22, and so on, do not get separated for meaning. Rather, they are to be looked at as a whole, single number.

PAY ATTENTION TO CONTEXT

What is the focus in your life right now? Your angel numbers aren't random: They target the main elements in your present experience. They are created to help move you along with the needed knowledge in whatever happiness or struggle you encounter. Reflecting on your current circumstances when receiving an angel number will help you understand what it pertains to.

Your angels will usually focus on one main theme at a time, and the numbers they send can pertain to pivotal moments, shifts in relationships, worries of today, or hard choices you may need to make. Grappling with a decision of selling a home, undergoing a difficult breakup, or being the main caregiver for a sick relative are all moments when your angels will step in to give support and wisdom in the form of number sequences.

LOOK TO LOCATION

Another way to interpret the meaning of your angel number is by considering location. Where did you see this number? Was it on the side of a building or on a license plate? Where were you, or where were you going when you saw it? Location is an important tool your angels use to communicate the meaning of a number, and it creates a way to personalize the message of that number for you. For example, seeing an angel number that you resonate with on an address of a home you are interested in buying can mean your search has ended.

Noticing numbers on your receipt from stopping to get coffee on your way to an important job interview can give you some insight into what mindset you should have when you enter that interview. Seeing a sequence on the wall in the hospital can give you some indication of what is to happen next. The following are key locations to consider when interpreting an angel number.

Numbers at Home

Are you finding yourself looking up at the clock at the same time every evening? Seeing your appliances flashing the same number as your recent utility bill? Repeatedly pausing your streaming show at the same time? Seeing numbers at home encourages you to center yourself. These messages are about you and your own connection to self and spirit; they are the most foundational messages.

Numbers at Work

The number of messages waiting for you in your voicemail, the order number you have to fulfill repeatedly, or the office number of a colleague you need to visit: Seeing a repetitive number sequence at work is indicative of the effect you have on others as you move through your life. Numbers in the workplace are messages that center on how you make the most of your time there, how you impact others, and how best to utilize your energy moving forward.

Numbers While Traveling or Commuting

The time of your flight, the gate of departure, a flashing sign on the road, the number of the exit you have to take: Numbers while you are traveling have a metaphorical meaning about your need to evolve and transcend your daily existence. Numbers in these contexts have a lot to do with changing things up, making tough choices, and thinking in the moment. They ask you to leave your comfort zone and move into the next phase of your journey to your higher self.

Numbers in Meaningful Places

The table number at the wedding you attend, the final score of the big game you're watching, the plot number of the grave you are about to visit at the cemetery: Repetitive number sequences in meaningful places are the angels' way of telling you to pay attention now. You are in the present moment the most in times of heightened emotions—the times you are making memories. These numbers capture your attention in these times in order to deliver powerful messages of who you are and what you are here to do. These messages are often transformative ones.

CONSIDER YOUR EMOTIONS

When you see an angel number, stop and check in with your immediate feelings. Be specific: Did it cause joy or sadness, a feeling of heaviness or hope? There are no wrong answers here. Your angels will infuse their numbers with emotional responses, which need to be taken into consideration when exploring their meaning. Feeling sad about seeing a number when you "should'" feel happy is meaningful, as is the opposite. You can feel calm or even giddy when you see an angel number. The feelings may be totally different than what you might expect when you see a number, and noticing that is part of unraveling the intended interpretation. Keep in mind that angel numbers are never intended to cause fear but are meant to help, inspire, and show support.

Feeling Confused

It's normal to feel confused at first, but there is no reason to stay confused for long. When you are unclear about the numbers presenting themselves to you, it's perfectly acceptable to ask your guides a follow-up question—they are expecting it! When you are feeling confused by a number, asking your angels something simple like "What does this mean?" or "What do I do next?" is how you take steps in utilizing a message to its fullest potential. You can meditate on your question, journal about it, or simply ask it aloud. Always ask your guides for further clarification when you need it, and even further repetition of the number. And believe it when you see it happen! Because your guides will deliver.

Feeling Awestruck

A number that stops you cold is no coincidence. Feeling awestruck is a tactic used by your angel guides to get you to not just see and pay attention to a message but also to *believe* it. Ask yourself what meanings such a number may have in your life. Important dates, old addresses, even numbers on a clock can have personal significance. When you see your old area code on a billboard, maybe it's time to pause and think about home, the past, and the road that brought you to where you are. When you see your late grandfather's birthday, stop to consider what he might have to say to you at this moment.

When a number attracts your attention and leads you to think about an associated event, person, or place, it's important to include that context in your interpretation.

Personalized Number Sequences

Your angels have a personal style, and when you heighten your bond with them, you'll become aware of it. Because of this, sometimes they will send unique number sequences that are complicated and therefore hard to explain without synchronicity. This is a number that is unique to you—and completely arbitrary. Think of sequences like 867, 362, or 157. Oftentimes this entirely random number sequence is one you've seen come up time and again. This angel "wink" number is different from all other angel number instances, as it's tailored just for you. Angel winks throw all the other rules out the window: They are your angel's specific way of saying "hello," and therefore they don't always mean anything more than that. You'll know a number is an angel wink number versus an angel message number because it will show up in all sorts of in-between and sideways moments randomly and concurrently throughout your whole life: your seat number at a concert, the number you see when you look up at the scoreboard of a ball game, the length of time of the call you just completed with a loved one.

Angel wink numbers can come in both good times and bad, whenever you are in need of support or encouragement. They are a reminder of sorts, that this life has a bigger meaning and that you are on the correct path. They are a universal way for your angels to show you the support system that eternally encircles you. The more you work with and notice angel numbers, the more likely you are to get your own angel wink! Your angels like to get your attention with these very special "calling card" number sequences.

HOW DO YOU USE ANGEL NUMBERS?

When you decode your angel numbers, you can start really using them to move your life (or continue on empowered) in the right direction. The following are ways to use your numbers to their full potential.

USING NUMBERS TO COMMUNICATE AND CONNECT WITH SPIRIT GUIDES

Angel number communication is a two-way street! Just as your angels can communicate with you in this way, you can do the same. Your angels are playful beings and enjoy when you call to them—and they will reciprocate in an equally creative and nuanced way. Notice the number sequences that are coming your way and begin to incorporate them into your life. When you see a number sequence that pops out at you continually, make sure to take a moment and honor it. A simple pause in your day to be present in the moment is all it takes to heighten your ability to get on the same vibration as the message at hand. Then you can start getting creative in how you use these numbers in a daily manner so as to pull the energy of their messages into your own reality.

USING NUMBERS TO MANIFEST

Part of the reason you receive angel numbers from your angels is to encourage you to make changes in your life for the better. Angel numbers call out to the universe through specific energies; you can use these numbers to harness those same energies and open up pathways to abundance. Choose a number that pops up for you often, or choose one from the codex in Part 2 that feels right for you. Angel numbers are a wonderful tool to help you create a reality that better suits your higher self!

Make a donation to an organization you love in the amount of an angel number. Use the numbers in your screen names for social media, email addresses, and even your passwords. Think of this as a "ping" you send out to your angels, so that they can then send a similar signal back to you. Using the numbers often in these little ways will heighten their frequency and raise your own vibration. The higher your vibration, the more messages you can receive!

USING NUMBERS IN MEDITATION

Numbers are patterns; they provide algorithms for how you set up your world, your reality, and your own plans. Meditating with your angel numbers can intensify their power in your life. Use your angel number as the amount of time you will meditate, and set a timer. Welcome the energy of that angel number in. Picture the number and remember the message it vibrates out into the universe. Opening yourself up to these frequencies is a way to create mindfulness. The more you welcome the messages of your angels in, the more opportunities they have to get your attention! You can meditate on the current joys or challenges you face or ask your angels to send you messages, support, and assistance.

RECORDING AND REFLECTING ON YOUR NUMBERS

As you look for, interpret, and use your angel numbers, you are building a method of communication with your angels. It's a lifelong process that will bring unprecedented clarity and personal growth. Recording your numbers in detail will assist in this process. You will begin to see patterns form, and you'll be able to look back and perceive the bigger picture of what your angels are repeatedly giving you. The patterns may seem small at first, but when seen together in greater numbers they fit so as to form a larger and more intricate message. On a more foundational level, reflecting on angel messages is essential for making use of them. When pondered, the numbers act as catalysts in your life. You will open up to new ideas, insights, and countless breakthroughs that will bring you closer to completing the objectives of your soul contract. Aligning with your higher self and the goals for being here brings untold peace and abundance into your life. You will begin recording your numbers in Part 3.

Part 2

THE NUMBERS CODEX

Numbers are everywhere, and once you start paying attention to them, your angels can really step up their communication with you! In the codex that follows, you will discover interpretations for angel numbers 0–999, as well as specific steps you can implement to reap the potential of each number in your own life. This codex will allow you to begin your journey of decoding the messages you are surrounded by. As you learned in Part 1, you can also use these numbers to call into your life the energies you wish to be surrounded by. The universe responds to you more effectively when you show it you are listening, and there is no better way to do that than to take the messages of angel numbers and incorporate them into daily life. You are learning the language of the angels, and in doing so, building a stronger relationship with your higher self and the goals you set forth here in your soul contract.

1. Architect

You have the ability to create.

Your world is shaped and altered by your thoughts and words. Right now you are creating, and the powerful forces of the universe are working with you. Remind yourself of this by repeating this mantra: "I am the universe, the universe is me."

2. Trust

**You build your life
with gratitude.**

It's not just the big things you can hope for; it's also the little things, which keep everything together. You are never alone, and your angels are reminding you that so many small things together create a miraculous and cumulative outcome. Create a list of what you are grateful for today.

3. Harmony

Mind, body, and spirit are one.

If something in your life is ignored or neglected, everything suffers. The health of the mind, body, and spirit connection is essential in living a fulfilled existence. This is the message from your angels today. Think of what you are doing to nurture all parts of you, and where you can do better at listening to the things you have neglected within.

4. Foundations

It's time to get back to basics.

There are things that, if left under-nurtured, can fall to ruin. Your angels remind you to go back to the foundations of self and take inventory of what is lacking. You can't build yourself up without maintaining all the good work you've already done. Journal today on one foundational part of your life that could use reinforcement.

5. Growth

The only thing that stays the same is change.

As the world around you shifts and moves, it's time to get flexible. Change is inevitable, and your peace comes not from the stability of things outside you, but also from that which is created from your foundation within. Your angels remind you to make inner peace a priority, so that when change comes, you know that you're tethered to something it cannot touch. Meditate today with a visualization of your inner peace tying you firmly to the universe.

6. Material World

Only love lasts eternally.

You are paying too much attention to the superficial. Oftentimes you can forget the depth of what you are doing in life by focusing on the material world's distractions. Your angels guide you to focus on the intangibles you have in your life—love, friendship, character qualities of self—and to give them a moment of appreciation.

7. Fear Not

Do not let fear control you.

Learning and growing come with new contexts and opportunities. You are feeling called to do new things without always knowing whom or what you can trust. Seeing this number reminds you to be spontaneous and courageous but also smart and cautious. It's okay to have a backup plan. When you see this number, create a list of what you are scared of and what you can do to mitigate those fears.

8. Abundance

The energy is limitless.

There are forces always flowing and moving through and around you. The ones you pay attention to and open up to will envelop you in their flow. When you see this number, meditate on what in your life requires development and abundance. Visualize energy coming forth to nurture growth in these areas.

9. Endings

The ending is a lesson.

In your life something is coming to completion. It can be sad and it's okay to mourn what was, but it's also important to recognize the lesson in this ending as well. Journal today on what you have learned, how you feel, and what you plan to do with this hard-won knowledge.

10. Clear Thinking

Cleanse your thoughts.

Angels are asking you to declutter your mind of things that are not necessary for your forward movement. Thoughts and emotions need to be productive, or else they can be problematic. Reflect upon a repetitive thought or emotion you've been having. Ask yourself if this thought or emotion is necessary, kind, and productive.

11. The Awakening

You are being called to attention.

Your angels want to send you signs, but first they need to make sure you'll be paying attention. This number asks you to notice the world around you so you don't miss the important messages coming your way. Ask your angels for confirmation after you see this number; repetition is their way of getting your attention!

12. Support

When you take the next step, you are not alone!

Life has sent you new opportunities, and now is the time to embrace them with the faith that you will be supported. The things that come your way are for your highest good. Reflect on how you've been helped by unseen forces in your life. Sit in the profound realization of how support comes in many forms.

13. Hope

Nurture yourself.

Your angels are aware you are going through a difficult time. They want you to put your energy into taking care of yourself. Plant a seed somewhere you can watch it grow. As you nurture this new life, you are nurturing your own as it gets acquainted with what surrounds you now.

14. Forward Thinking

You're planting the seeds for your future.

That vision you hold dear for your future is being nurtured today. The work you put in will be rewarded. Write down your vision in great detail. Visualize yourself reading it again after it's been realized.

15. New Ideas

Level up your thoughts.

Inspiration is the way your angels are directing you onto your inspired path. The ideas you get are important as they lead you to the next step. Repeat this mantra: "I am open to receiving divine inspiration."

16. Be Yourself

There is only one you.

The journey you are on is to be yourself, not to be anyone else. Your angels encourage you to stop comparing yourself to others. Write a poem or a song, or create a piece of art that represents your unique experience as you.

17. Aspire

Think bigger!

Your angels encourage you to speak your wants and dreams aloud to the universe. Get creative with what you want, and see it happening in great detail. Visualize an experience in which you receive something you always wanted; feel thankful for it as if it has already happened.

18. Wish

Manifest your desires.

It's brave to want something, and your angels are asking you to be very brave. Make a wish and let it out into the universe, knowing it will come back to you in divine timing! Write down a wish and set it out where the wind can carry it away from you. As it flies away, you will know your angels have it now.

19. Take Care

Show yourself love.

In your smallest actions today, reflect self-love. In every action you carry out, understand that the universe will reflect it back in others' actions toward you. Create a to-do list of loving things you'll do for yourself as you go about your day; carry it with you and check it often!

20. Gratitude

Boost your energy levels.

Being thankful for what you have aligns you with divine light and love. Your angels want you to focus on that today and feel good while doing it. Pen a letter to your future self, describing what you have presently that makes you feel grateful.

21. Advancement

You are about to level up!

The next step is coming, so prepare yourself to receive it. Think of what you need to release in order to do so. Write it down, and at the next full moon either burn it or bury it and feel the space open up for what is next.

22. Believe

You are building the life you want.

Your angels are in direct communication with you. This number is a powerful message that your life is being created with their divine assistance. You are in a space of high-vibrational energy right now! Repeat this mantra: "I believe in myself as I grow."

23. Philanthropy

What can you do for others?

This number calls upon you to ask yourself how you can contribute to society. Be what you want to receive, and channel unconditional love as you do so. Think of an organization or person who could use your time. Make a plan to help!

24. Goal Setting

What you want should reflect who you are.

When you are setting goals, your angels remind you that they must be authentic to you. Where in your life might you be doing things that sound good to others but not yourself? Review your goals today, and make sure they feel in line with your soul journey.

25. Major Decision

You already know what to do.

Your soul is calling out for change, and you will have to make a choice as to how to go about that. Have confidence that in your heart, you already know the answer. Repeat this mantra: "I will make the right decisions at the right time."

26. Money Flows

Money is energy; prepare yourself to receive it!

Abundance is coming to you in all forms, and one way it can present itself is financially. Gratitude creates the clearest pathway to you. Sit in meditation today and reflect with a grateful heart on all that you already have been blessed with in life.

27. Life Plan

Align your life plan with your soul plan.

Your angels want you to reflect and consider deeply what it is you want in life versus what you think you should do. Create alone time for yourself today without people or technology. Ask yourself what you want and freewrite about it in a journal without judgment.

28. See Worth

Make what you have enough.

You have been asking for what you want, but your angels want you to look around and really appreciate what you already have. Gratitude creates abundance. Create a list in your journal today starting with "I am grateful for..." and include everything you can think of!

29. Center

Hold on to your purpose.

When the swirling forces of life distract you, remember what your goals are. You have a reason to be here; focus on that, and all will be well. Lie down and place your hands on your solar plexus chakra (just above the navel). Repeat this mantra: "I have a purpose."

30. Trilogy

Mind, body, and spirit grow stronger together.

Your efforts to strengthen the bond between these parts of you are fortifying your connection with the divine and creating a brilliant reality! Nurture all parts of yourself today in a ritual of connection. Meditate and picture a brilliant white light running through you, creating links and pathways of communication between mind, body, and spirit.

31. Work

Your life needs your action.

In order to get your life in motion, you need to take action. Your angels are reminding you that your dreams and goals are worthy, and to achieve them, you have to put in some work. List a goal you have and three actions you can take today to support it. Get at least one thing checked off your list before the day is done!

32. Invest

In all that you do, invest your whole self.

Your angels remind you that by investing your whole self into the microcosm, the macrocosm eventually reflects that effort. In a small chore, job, or interaction today, feel the presence of the divine as you treat that activity as if it were a blueprint for creating a larger representation of your reality.

33. Love and Peace

You are never alone.

Your angels are with you, listening and receiving your prayers. But they want you to stretch a little further. What can you do to help yourself today? Reflect on a present problem and think of one way to make it slightly less difficult. No matter how small the action, it matters!

34. Creative Connection

You have a spark!

You are being called to pay close attention to the energies that drive you and motivate you. Get excited about creating your own life by following creative pursuits. Create a vision board with images and words that capture your attention and resonate deep within you.

35. Supportive Bonds

Build your relationship with the spiritual.

Throughout the winds of change, your angels acknowledge they are here to support you. Building a relationship with them will strengthen this bond. Pen a letter to your angels asking them to reveal themselves to you with unique signs and symbols.

36. Resources

You are your best asset!

It's time to jump into the next chapter with confidence that the skills and knowledge you already possess are going to be enough. Create a list of all the skills you bring to the table in a relationship, job, or new project.

37. Independent

Try it yourself.

There is something in your life that you could do on your own. You are being given confidence from your angels—use it. Think of where you may have become unnecessarily dependent on others for help, and start trying it on your own.

38. Give Back

Pay it forward.

Your angels want you to share your blessings with those less fortunate than you. Paying your fortune forward is how you can do this. Choose a person or place today that you can give your time or money to.

39. Career

Make sure your job and soul align!

There is a need for you to feel fulfilled with the work you do every day. Your angels are asking you to align your career goals with your soul contract. What job change can you make in order to do that? Revisit your resume today to see how you've grown.

40. Reassurance

It's all going to be okay.

The choices you've made, the place you are presently, and the direction you are going in are all angel approved! Your soul journey is happening as planned. Practice a grounding exercise today—sit out in the sun and place your bare feet on the earth, or take a salt bath.

41. Wishes Made

Hope is faith that in divine timing, you'll get what you need.

Your angels want you to discard a specific timeline for the arrival of what you want. Wish for those things to come, but detach from how and when they do. Write down something you feel stressed about presently and bury the paper as a symbolic gesture that good things will grow in time.

42. Stay Involved

You are the most invested!

The present situation around you needs your direct involvement. Your angels are discouraging you from handing it off to someone who won't care the way you do. How can you stay engaged in a way that helps everything stay on track?

43. Look Ahead

Make a plan for the future.

Goals and dreams are essential, and your angels are asking you to create them now. Show the universe you are invested! Spend time today outlining specific goals you have and steps you can take to achieve them.

44. Divine Intervention

Ask for protection.

The angelic realm is around you presently. The angels want you to ask them for help and support with stronger intentions. Lie in meditation today and repeat this mantra: "I am ready for divine intervention in my life."

45. Look Up

Things are coming together.

Life can seem like many scattered pieces at present, but rest assured, those pieces are very much interconnected. Look at the overlap today, and see where things are coming together. Several times throughout the day repeat this mantra: "I trust in the plan for my life."

46. The Prize

Don't lose sight of what's important.

Your angels validate that distractions in the material world can produce disconnect from self and spirit. Show the universe you know where your priorities lie today by doing something that shows you keep your eyes on the prize!

47. Procrastination

Get to work!

Putting off what you have to do is not working. Your angels are giving you the fortitude to move through a task efficiently and without distraction. Several times throughout the day repeat this mantra: "I can do anything." Then get to work.

48. Intention-Setting

You get what you ask for.

Your angels are indicating that you've entered a period when it's very easy to get what you ask for. The pathways are clear. Write down an intention today that is reflective of your authentic self and place it somewhere you will see it often.

49. Closure

Say goodbye.

A present situation in your life requires your ability to put closure on it. Lie in meditation and visualize what you need closure on. See yourself saying goodbye and coming to peace with not always understanding all the reasons why something happened the way it did, knowing you can have peace from the lessons it brought you.

50. Loving Mindset

Prioritize all love.

Your angels ask you to make changes in your life to accommodate all forms of love. Self, familial, and romantic love are being channeled to you. Lie in meditation with your hands on your heart chakra. Repeat this mantra: "I am love."

51. Take Initiative

Make your own magic.

The time is right for you to make your own way forward. Waiting for things to happen isn't working; it's time to make your own magic! Today, get moving on a goal or project that propels your life into the next phase.

52. Fine-Tuning
Hone your skills.

You are being called not just to pass on certain skills, but also to really focus on them and make them the best they can be. An interest you have is calling to you for more attention. Acknowledge this and create a plan for furthering your own education on the matter.

53. Self-Control
React accordingly.

The power lies in you to gain control over your responses in a present situation. Your angels call on you to feel solid in your ability to react appropriately to the challenges in front of you. Several times today repeat this mantra: "I am in control of how I respond."

54. Failure
Missteps redirect you to an authentic path!

A recent event did not go as planned, and your angels want you to work on not being hard on yourself in the aftermath. Write a journal honestly exploring your emotional state today, and reflect on how mistakes happen so we can learn something.

55. Change
Things will look different!

When you ask for what you want, your angels deliver. And that time is on its way. You are being told that your intentions are being taken seriously. Lie in meditation with your hands over your root chakra (the base of the spine). Repeat this mantra: "I am ready for what is next."

56. Proactive Thoughts

Focus on success.

Circumstances in your life are getting a needed change. Things are looking up. Today, focus on your successes more than your failures. While it's important to acknowledge both, spend a little more time noticing the things that go right today, instead of those that go wrong.

57. New Approach

Strive for clarity.

The way you are looking at things is being lovingly challenged. The doors that keep closing around you are doing so because you need a new approach. Today, ask your angels for clarity and reflect on how to get what you want in a different way.

58. Turning Point

Life will look different.

The place you are at is both an end and a beginning: It's a turning point. From this moment on, life will look different. Compose a letter to your future self. Describe your current situation, including your feelings and emotional state.

59. Profound

A spiritual awakening occurs.

Your angels validate that you have had a profound realization in your life. Because of this you are now walking on a new spiritual plane. Your soul has been heard, and you are aligning your life with its calling. Spend time in meditation today, taking in divine light.

60. Be Prosperous

**Find love and harmony
at home!**

The message today is about creating an abundance of harmony in your house, so that its effects reverberate outward into all areas of your life. Your angels want you to build a foundation for a prosperous life. Plan an activity that focuses on family, home, and harmony today.

61. Love

Demonstrate love in action.

There are many ways to show your love to the people in your life, and your angels want you to do that today. Listen to someone thoughtfully, keep a promise you made, or make someone you appreciate feel important. Do something to make others feel your love.

62. Acquisition

**Prepare for the arrival
of what is new!**

Your angels want you to acquire all that is in your highest good, but in order to do so, you must let go of the reluctance to give up the old ways of doing things. Repeat this mantra: "I am willing to become the version of myself that is the most authentic."

63. Be Reliable

**Prove yourself
through challenges.**

Your world is increasingly filled with challenges, all of which are here to serve your highest good. It's a wonderful opportunity to demonstrate reliability. Today, reflect on what it means to be reliable and write a list of ways you are currently doing this, as well as places in your life where you could work on this.

64. Intent

State what you want to accomplish.

Your angels ask you to state out loud what you intend to accomplish. This could be an intention for the day or a much broader life intention. Either way, write it down and post it where you can see it often. Repeat it to yourself throughout the day!

65. Transformation

Your efforts produce change!

The efforts you've made toward living your authentic life are not for nothing. Your angels encourage you to see how your personal transformation is creating a mirrored effect in your reality. Observe parallels today between your own self-growth and what has changed in your daily life.

66. Responsibility

Create your own response.

Even though your life can present many challenges, people, and situations that are out of your control, how you respond to them is always your choice. You are being asked to reflect on the small ways you can keep your responses as choices you make rather than automatic reactions.

67. Enlightenment

Wake up.

Your soul is waking up, and it's bringing your reality with it! Your angels want you to practice enlightenment in your everyday life to support your soul's growth. Be in the present moment today; tune in to your bodily sensations and acknowledge your emotional state without judgment. Simply "be."

68. Spiritually Organize

Self-assess your happiness.

Your angels are asking you to get spiritually organized! Today, take an honest assessment of your life. Write down what areas you do and do not feel organized in. Narrow it down to the hours in a day, so as to reflect on where little changes can be made to ease discomfort.

69. New Cycles

Accept and adapt.

The natural order of things is change, and your angels are alerting you to the new cycles beginning presently. You are being encouraged to work on acceptance of what is, and focus on adaptability rather than seeing this change as a setback. Repeat this mantra: "I am adaptable."

70. Inner Wisdom

Source energy is yours!

The answers to your questions are not outside you—rather, they are within. You are being reminded by your angels that you are tapped in to source energy (the all-encompassing energy of the universe itself), and it is abundant and limitless. When a question arises today, take a moment to answer it yourself first before turning to an external source.

71. Spiritual Goals

Feel the sacred energy within you.

Your life is full of goals that reflect the material world, but this number is a message to set spiritual goals as well. Today, your angels ask you to create a list of what you want to expound more on in your connection to the divine.

72. Quality

Align your life to your soul!

You are being asked to align your life in a way that authentically reflects your soul. The desires you have are perhaps simpler than the life you lead. What can you do today to facilitate quality in all your environments and relationships rather than quantity?

73. Overcome Challenges

There is opportunity for growth.

The universe is sending you a multitude of moments that are going to transform you! Challenges such as these are not necessarily negative when you can view them as opportunities for personal growth. Write about a present challenging moment in life and how you can perceive it as useful for growth.

74. Stay Focused

You are following the right path.

Your angels are showing you that your soul contract is aligned with your current life trajectory. Staying focused on your goals is all you need to do now. Meditate today on an intention you have set that is close to your heart.

75. Dream Big

Change your life for the better!

You are being asked to focus on your wildest dream today. Create a vision board for what you want. Then list ten steps backward from that goal. Place your vision board somewhere you will see it often and check off the steps one at a time.

76. Spiritual Awakening

Process new thoughts.

You are being awakened from the material world into the spiritual one. As the thoughts and emotions you have merge with your higher self, it can become overwhelming to process the new insights you gain. Lie in meditation with your hands on your crown chakra (the top of the head), and repeat this mantra: "I receive!"

77. Calm Fears

You are supported!

The fears you have may not go anywhere anytime soon, but they don't have to control you. Your angels are reassuring you that they give you their full support. Work on calming your fears today by taking a bath, going on a nature walk, or simply enjoying a cup of tea.

78. Abundance Mindset

Share with others who will pay it forward.

Your angels want you to embrace the universal truth that there is plenty of money, power, and recognition in the world to share with others. Give some of your time or resources to a person or organization you know can benefit today.

79. Heart Listening

Emotions don't lie!

You are being encouraged by your angels to lead with your emotions when facing a present situation. Making yourself do something you don't want to do is not the answer. Sit with your feelings today and sort out what needs to be done versus what can wait.

80. Receive

Accept the gifts of the universe.

As you work toward a common goal, open your hands to the gifts the universe wants to bestow on you. Visualize with your meditation today that you are receiving a beautiful gift. Simply hold this image in a state of gratitude and say, "Thank you."

81. Guidance

You are led by divine wisdom!

You have an inherent ability to connect with the divine, and your angels are asking you to tap in to this. The present situation requires you to navigate according to your inner guidance. Lie with your hands on your crown chakra (the top of the head). Repeat this mantra: "I am led by divine wisdom."

82. Invite Creativity

Try something new.

You are being encouraged to invite creativity into your life today. Being creative in this sense doesn't mean you are good at any one thing; it means you are adventurous enough to try things from different angles and perspectives. Pick up a creative pursuit today and let your mind flow differently!

83. Ownership

Take responsibility.

You have the ability to change your life by changing your thoughts and subsequent reactions. Think about how you can take ownership of your emotions, thoughts, and actions toward everything you do today. Contemplate how you can own an emotion, thought, or action that you previously disregarded.

84. Let Go

There is a need to let go of a person or situation at this time.

Your angels acknowledge the many doubts and worries that fill your head. They encourage you not to second-guess your intuition and hold on to something that doesn't serve you. Sit in meditation today and visualize your life without this person or thing in it; is your life better?

85. Spiritual Shift

You have a choice.

The changes around you are inevitable. You have the choice to make them positive. Your angels ask you, as challenging as it may feel, to find one thing you can make better in your life in the midst of all of these shifts. Journal about how you can activate positive change.

86. People Pleasing

Your voice is your own!

Your angels understand that you seek acceptance from others, but they caution you today against pleasing everyone. Not only is it impossible, but you are also losing your own voice in your attempts. Lie in meditation with your hands on your throat chakra. Repeat this mantra: "My voice is my own; my voice is strong."

87. Align Yourself

Get on the same vibe.

Getting what you want requires you to be on the same vibrational frequency as that thing. Your angels are asking you to practice becoming that which you want. Prepare yourself within to not just attract the thing you most desire but to also become it. Repeat this mantra: "I align with my desires."

88. Welcome Riches

State your intention.

Infinite abundance is available to you, and your angels are signaling for you to remember this. They want you to elevate your vibration, as well as your expectations for what you can receive. Write down an intention you have for the future. State it out loud under the stars during the next new moon!

89. Heal Others

You can sense others' feelings as clearly as your own.

Your angels validate that you are a highly sensitive being. Volunteer some time in something you feel drawn to, help out someone who otherwise wouldn't ask for aid but can benefit from it, or read up on other ways to turn your empathy into action.

90. The Close

Let go of what no longer serves you.

There is a significant ending happening in one part of your life right now. Your angels validate its significance. However, you are being urged to let it go and find closure. Lie in meditation and repeat this mantra: "I let go of what no longer serves me."

91. Embrace Newness

You can do anything!

There is a new life ahead of you, and it's yours to take right now. Your angels are encouraging you to embrace whatever it is, knowing it's in your highest good. Lie in meditation with your hands on your solar plexus chakra (just above the navel). Repeat this mantra: "I can do anything."

92. Feel

Honor what was.

Moving on after a loss you've recently experienced is not easy, and your angels validate and support you in this journey. Spend time feeling your feelings in the authentic way they present themselves to you. Use a journal to record these emotions.

93. Career Change

Positive transitions are ahead.

There is change in the air when it comes to your career! Your angels ask you to embrace this time of transition and focus on the excitement and opportunity that lie ahead. Repeat this mantra: "I embrace positive changes in my life."

94. Be Success

Celebrate yourself!

Your angels acknowledge that you've struggled long and hard to come to this moment. Success is yours to receive. Recognize where in your life you are successful; there is nothing too small to congratulate yourself about today.

95. Adventure

Seek adventure in your daily life.

Your angels want you to stir up passion and inspiration by finding things that make you excited. Plan something today to look forward to. Explore a new hiking trail or navigate a new road with a paper map, and discover something new in your world!

96. Self-Awareness

Be honest with yourself.

Being honest about your own strengths and weaknesses is what your angels are calling you to do today. Create time to embrace a heightened sense of self-awareness. Notice the pattern in which you conduct yourself and interact with others, and how cohesive your self-talk is with your actions.

97. Unity

Unite your voice with others!

You are asked to join your voice in unity with others to create compassionate and needed change. Ask yourself where you feel pulled to assist with helping for the greater good, and take a step toward that today.

98. Be Generous

Being giving is good for others and yourself!

Your angels want you to level up your life satisfaction by giving to others today. Be generous with your time by helping someone out, with your heart by giving compassion, or with your belongings by sharing what you have.

99. Completion

Accept the changes to come.

There is a completion happening in your life. It's time to reflect on the lessons of the past so as to prepare for what is to come. Endings can be painful, but your angels support you. Repeat this mantra: "I accept positive change in my life."

100. Authentic Life

Live your truth.

You have infinite potential. In order to align with your authentic path you must make choices that reflect who you are. Your angels are giving you encouragement to live authentically. Today, journal about what living your truth looks like for you.

101. Mood Matters

Any feeling is a good one.

It's normal to want to feel happy all the time, but that's not realistic. Your angels are giving you assurance that all your emotions, no matter what they are, are important. Emotions are meant to be explored and learned from. List three feelings you have three times a day for the next three days. Do not judge yourself or try to shift these feelings; simply explore them.

102. Address Problems

Let go of unnecessary situations.

Your angels want you to sort out which problems are yours and which are not. You are not in charge of the problems others put upon you unnecessarily. Write a list of which problems you presently feel responsible for, and narrow the list down to what you can solve for yourself.

103. Self-Worth

Be loving.

You are your best asset, and it's time to form a daily routine that reflects that. Your angels support you prioritizing your self-care. Invest in some skin care, take regular walks, and eat your greens! Remind yourself and the universe that you are worthy of love.

104. Values

Align your choices to who you are.

The values you have need to be incorporated into every choice you make. Present circumstances can make it easy to ignore what's authentic to you in favor of a quick result. Your angels encourage you to take a moment to reflect before acting, so as to make a decision that aligns to who you are.

105. Inner Voice

Listen to yourself.

The guidance you need to cultivate is your own. Your inner voice is speaking, and your angels are calling you to listen carefully. Lie in meditation, clear your mind, and ask your higher self to assist with your connection to this voice.

106. Image

Focus within.

Currently there is much focus on your own image, material surroundings, and superficial identity. Your angels ask you to delve deeper and, in doing so, facilitate a higher degree of focus on your connection with self and spirit. Write down the things in your life you value that have no material form to them.

107. Embrace Fear

Get comfortable within.

It's normal to have fears when it comes to completing your goals. Your angels want you to befriend these feelings! In time you'll see that while they may not go away, they don't have to control you. Write down your current fears, and reflect on how to challenge them in small ways.

108. Learn

Useful lessons are coming to you!

Every experience is an opportunity to learn and grow. As much as it may sting right now, the lessons you are receiving are priceless. Your angels encourage you to write down what you feel now, and how you will utilize what you are learning to help you in the future.

109. Starting Over

A chapter has ended.

There is a time in your life to start over, and that time is now. A chapter has closed on one part of your life, but a new one has already begun. Write a letter to your future self relating all the feelings and thoughts you have right now.

110. It's Personal

Your journey is unique.

It's easy to look around and be distracted by others' personal journeys and endeavors in life, but today the angels call on you to focus on only your own. Comparing your path to the paths of others is not the way forward. Today, take a moment to meditate on your own personal path to the divine and in what ways you've grown along the way.

111. Screenshot

Pause and reset your thinking.

When you see 111, think of the universe as taking a "screenshot" of your frame of mind right now. Everything that is going on—all your thoughts, feelings, goals, and dreams—is going to be replicated. Get on a high vibe quickly, so you can manifest your best life moving forward. Repeat the mantra: "I am in alignment with my authentic self."

112. Love Abounds

Love unlocks all doors.

When you look in the right places, you will find that love exists everywhere. Your angels call upon you to envelop yourself in the forces of unconditional love in order to manifest your highest goals. Visualize a light covering your entire being, filling you with the powerful forces of the universe and making you one with the divine. When you do this, you will feel loved.

113. Breakaway

You cannot start anew without letting something go.

Your angels ask you to reframe this time not as an ending but as a new beginning. They ask you to create high vibrations by welcoming change. Pay attention to what is awakening in you. Journal about something that excites you at this time.

114. Don't Stop

You're almost there— push ahead!

In your life, your angels recognize you are exhausted. There is still some work to do, and they implore you to keep going. Take a small break, but pick it up again! Take a salt bath and visualize all the stress leaving your body.

115. Choose Love

When in doubt, follow your heart.

Your guides want to send you love because you are worthy of it. Open yourself up to receiving self-love, romantic love, and familial love by cleansing your heart chakra: Place rose quartz over your heart and ask your angels to clear any blockages you may have.

116. Comparison

**Don't look around,
only within.**

Your angels remind you that comparing yourself to others only takes away from your own beautiful experience. What do you feel you are lacking? Journal your answer as a letter directly to your angels. Know they will receive this correspondence and respond to you with signs.

117. Write It

Create your new reality.

Ask for what you want, and believe it is coming to you in divine timing. Light a candle and write down your deepest wishes and desires. Focus on each one as you list it. When you are done, give gratitude to your angels for their support in creating your new reality.

118. Abundant Love

**Love abundantly
surrounds you.**

You are being woken up to see the truth: that love has always been around you and always will be. And because you see this now, more love can arrive! Look for new love all around you, and be open to its presence in your life in any form it enters in.

119. Shifts

Change your patterns.

What can you do to make today feel just a little different? Your angels want you to switch up a pattern in your life for the better. Plan an impromptu visit to a friend, drive home from work a more scenic way, or eat something new for lunch!

120. Moon Magic

What is it that you want to improve?

Your angels ask you to look within and set an intention that serves your highest good. Write it on a piece of paper, and, during the next new moon, light a white candle and state your intention out loud. With the power of your words you will release it into the universe.

121. Healing

You are repairing yourself.

The wounds are still healing, but your angels are with you during this time. They want you to know that someday, it won't hurt as much as it does today. Spend some time with innocent creatures today: children, animals, or anyone who has pure love in their heart. Feel the unconditional love of the divine when you look in their eyes.

122. Look Around

Your prayers are manifesting.

You are being called to look around and see what is coming your way. There have been many changes around you so as to create room for the things you are manifesting. Create a list of the things that seem different in your life presently; reflect on how they are the result of your prayers.

123. Stepping Stones

You are on your way!

You are on a distinct path, and are well on your way to your goals. Little things matter. Pay attention to the details, as each choice you make presents a small part of the big picture. Visualize a path in front of you leading you to your heart's desire.

124. Review

Little moments matter.

As you set goals in your life, know that with every thought, word, and subsequent action, you are creating it. Review your goals today and reflect on how the little moments in your daily life have power and influence over the creation of the larger picture.

125. Be Serious

Invest in yourself first.

Your angels are reminding you that your interests and goals must be taken seriously. If you put them on the back burner, the universe will too. Reaffirm your commitment to yourself by repeating this mantra: "I am worthy."

126. Understand

Prioritize your spiritual mindset.

Your angels warn you of the danger of focusing too much on this material world. They urge you to shift your priorities to your spiritual connection. Connect to the divine by lying in meditation. Visualize a light shining through your crown chakra (the top of the head), and repeat this mantra: "I understand how to align with the divine."

127. Creation

You are creating your soul's plan.

The choices you've made are in line with your soul contract. Feel assured that the path you take presently is leading you to where you want to be. Create an intention today that aligns you further to the divine's plan for you. Write it down and place it where you can see it every day!

128. Thankfulness

Practice gratitude in every moment.

In little moments, take the time to be thankful. As you cook, do household chores, drive, or even fold laundry, use the time to speak to your angels and let them know all the things you are thankful for in this moment.

129. Peaceful Room

Create a sacred space in your home.

The outside world can distract you, so to stay on track, you must create peace within. Use a corner of a room, a bathroom, or a spot in your garden to create a place for meditation, prayer, and contemplation.

130. Creator

You create what you see.

The balance in your life will reflect itself in every relationship and opportunity you encounter. Work on balance in yourself to produce balance in your environment. In a safe place, try out some balancing postures for a few moments today. Breathe through them, and repeat this mantra: "I am steady."

131. Growing

Honor your growth!

The respect of the mind, body, and spirit connection are leading you to your goals. Create a self-care activity that nurtures all parts of yourself today. Take a contemplative walk in nature, swim in a body of water, or spend time studying something that interests you.

132. Divine Rituals

In all you do, feel wholly present.

Your world is manifesting right now, and the way it is doing this is by watching your investment in the little things you do every day. Think of your daily chores, jobs, and interactions today as divine rituals.

133. Channel Divinity

Be someone's angel.

There is a person who needs your unconditional love and assistance. What is a selfless act you can provide today that will help this person feel the divine in themselves and around them? Channel your angels and be inspired to help another person.

134. It Resonates

Your soul is aligning to its purpose!

Pay attention to the times you feel enthusiastic chills running through you and look forward to what is coming. Get in the habit of stopping yourself when you feel excited today; ask yourself to take a deeper look.

135. Self-Connect

Create a daily ritual.

Connecting to self and spirit each day will further your ability to manifest a life that aligns to your authentic self and soul plan. Spend at least fifteen minutes each day doing this. A nature walk, coffee outside with the birds, or quiet meditation are all small examples of what you can do for your self and spirit today.

136. Trailblazer
Use what you've got!

You have what you need to get where you are going. Nourish your most fulfilling life with the confidence that you are resourceful and creative. Lie in meditation with your hands on your sacral chakra (the lower stomach). Repeat this mantra: "I am creative."

137. Bigger Picture
Your world is your doing!

You are creating your own world. This number is a reminder from your angels that you are the one creating, so you have to make choices every day that reflect the bigger picture. Create a vision board with images and words that inspire you.

138. Core Values
Revisit your core values.

The values you hold dear can get buried under the distractions of present complications. Your angels ask you to uncover and revisit them. List your core beliefs and character qualities. Meditate on them today, visualizing their growth and strong connection to the divine.

139. Achieve
Your success helps others!

Your angels want you to embrace your soul's purpose within a career rather than your ego's necessity of it. Think of how your contributions can help others, and brainstorm how you could level up in order to provide that needed assistance.

140. Imprint

Today's mindset magnifies!

The mindset you carry today is under a microscope of the cosmos. It is being imprinted and magnified for your future reality. Take care today not to control the events around you but instead to control your responses to them. Stop frequently throughout the day and do a feelings and thoughts reflection and reset!

141. Chances

Demonstrate faith in self!

Your angels understand that it's risky to try for something you really want, and that the disappointment of not getting it can be hard. It's not about what you get, however, but rather the faith you demonstrate in yourself by going for it. Repeat this mantra: "I am confident."

142. Outcome

The work you put in today affects the overall outcome.

Your angels are urging you to stay involved and invested in a current project. Your positive attention is necessary. Take an extra step today in order to demonstrate interest in how this project plays out in the long run.

143. You Create

Reflect on past goals.

The world around you has been created by your past goals and dreams! The manifestations of the past are everywhere. Your angels want you to notice them today. Contemplate how a past goal has materialized and is now part of your daily life.

144. Connect

Communicate with the divine.

Making the connection with the divine in your daily life is exactly what your angels are urging you to do. They want to strengthen your ability to communicate on a high-vibrational level. Lie in meditation with your hands on your crown chakra (the top of the head), and repeat this mantra: "I am connected."

145. Cohesion

Create harmony.

The many parts of your life that seemingly don't interconnect actually do! What can you do to further the cohesion of all areas of your life so as to create harmony? Brainstorm a way to connect one area of your life to another, sharing your energy to benefit both places!

146. Self-Talk

You manifest what you dwell upon.

The number 146 is a timely reminder to revisit your self-talk, mantras, and how you speak about yourself to others. The ways you use these tools create the reality you are living in. Today, closely monitor all forms of expression either to yourself or about yourself. Observe where you can use some fine-tuning!

147. Demonstrate Diligence

Show the universe your appreciation.

Show the universe you are respectful of your time and energy by diligently addressing the tasks ahead of you today. How you treat what the universe gives you will provide a blueprint for what comes next! Repeat this mantra: "I move through tasks with efficiency." Then get to work!

148. Higher Power
Speak your intentions.

The universe is providing for you, and it's time to state your clear intentions to a higher power. Today, light a white candle and write an intention reflective of your authentic self. Speak it out loud to your angels. Place the written intention somewhere you can see it often.

149. The Narrative
Restart today!

Your narrative needs some reworking! Your angels want you to bring your attention to the stories you tell yourself. Rework the narrative using statements that reflect your truth and focus on the positive life lessons that you have learned.

150. Be Love
To get it, be it!

Whether you are single or in a relationship, your angels are urging you to create more love in your life. Create and strengthen love bonds. Speak with loving words about yourself and others, and extend a loving smile or gesture to those around you.

151. Make Magic
Your desires are in your hands!

The things you want are not just going to happen: You'll be the one to create them! The steps you take today have a direct link to what happens to you in the future. Create a plan to make some magic in your own life, right now.

152. Forward

You are being led to what is next!

The skill you are currently working on is the bridge by which you will pass into the next chapter of your life. Lie down and visualize where this bridge is leading you, and what it will look like when you get there.

153. Inner Strength

Positive results are ahead!

Your angels are applauding your recent focus on self-discipline. The toxic things you say no to produce positive results in the long run. You are telling the universe you are worth the effort it takes today to live your best life tomorrow. Repeat this mantra: "I have strong inner strength."

154. Personal Journey

Valuable lessons have been learned.

The journey you have begun is a result of your choosing to learn valuable lessons from past mistakes. Your angels are proud of your personal journey of self-truth and personal responsibility. Write a list of what you have changed in your life since learning a valuable lesson.

155. Accomplishment

You are rewarded!

The work you've done is being rewarded on many levels. Intentions you've made are being taken by your angels and manifested for you. The accolades you receive presently are an indication that more are to come. Thank your angels by doing something to help another person today.

156. Personal Truths

Rewrite the story.

You are what you think you are, and your angels want you to shift that narrative. People might tell you who or what you are, but what they say is not necessarily true. Think of something you get told a lot about your personality, and reflect on its truth in your life.

157. New Mindset

Change your view!

Your angels want you to see how new perspectives contribute to living authentically. Do something today that alters your perspective. Rearrange your furniture, listen to different music, or strike up a conversation with a new person.

158. The Grind

Stamina creates abundance.

Success is just around the corner. Your angels encourage you to keep stamina up today so as to show faith in the final outcome. Today, think of the hardest thing you know you have to do, and get that done first!

159. Thoughts

Observe your mind.

You have had a realization that thoughts are to be observed, not blindly followed. The mindfulness you are demonstrating is what will profoundly shift your life in a direction that is soul-aligned. Write about a thought you repeatedly have, reflecting on what observations you can make about it.

160. Turn Inward

External issues are solved within.

The solutions to the lack of abundance in your life lie within you! Journal today on where you have denied yourself vital elements for your mental, physical, and spiritual health. How does this neglect translate to your external reality?

161. Certitude

No one is perfect!

Your angels remind you that no one in your life is perfect, and from time to time they may disappoint you. But your angels want you to have certainty in the ones you love. It is about believing you are confident enough to handle a disappointment. Have a conversation with someone close to you about why you trust them.

162. Improvements

Change brings abundance.

You are being reminded through the number 162 that without a present change, things cannot get better for you! Your angels ask you to shift your perspective and see how things that are going away are leaving room for the new and improved to show up. Repeat this mantra: "I look forward to the future!"

163. Self-Reliance

Manage your own life.

While at times it's necessary to depend on others, there are places where you do not need to. Create a list of things in your life you can do today to be more self-reliant! Start by taking control over a small chore, making a choice on your own, or solving a problem independently.

164. Activate Intentions

Write them down.

You are being called to put your intentions out into the universe! Your angels alert you that the universe is ready to activate them! Write down what you intend to accomplish on a piece of paper. Under the stars during the next new moon, state your intention out loud.

166. Don't Wait

Go get what you want!

You must be the one who makes the move to get the things you want. Your angels are here to support you, but that doesn't mean everything is going to be handed to you without your effort. Take initiative today toward one of your goals—big or small, your effort matters.

165. Personal Growth

Challenges are opportunities!

It's all how you see it, and your angels encourage you to see every challenge you currently face as an opportunity to become more authentic. Take time today to see how a challenge you face is a way for you to cultivate personal growth.

167. Wake Up

Mindfulness is key.

You are being called to begin a lifetime practice of mindfulness. The world around you, and how it interacts with you, requires thoughtful attention, as there are signs and signals everywhere that can become catalysts for your spiritual growth. Start by journaling your observations of self in this very moment. Create a daily habit of reflecting in this way.

168. Honest Assessment

Set yourself up for success.

The places in your day that give you joy—and the ones that do not—need an honest assessment. From there, action needs to be taken to alter those things that are not serving you. Choose a part of your daily routine that could use some reorganization so as to set yourself up for more long-term success.

169. Nourish Intentions

Start this off right!

The forthcoming changes in your life cannot be controlled, so your angels ask you to be proactive instead. State an intention you want to set forward in your life. Write it down and bury it in a pot of soil along with a seed. As you nurture the growing life of the seed, know that your intention is also nourished.

170. Present Moment

Make time to notice messages.

You are getting many messages from your angels, and they are asking you to be present to notice them. They note that your life is busy lately, and it's interfering with your connection to the divine. Take a look at your schedule today and carve out some time to be present.

171. Small Improvements

Raise the vibe!

Your angels ask you to focus on how you can leave everything you interact with better than how you found it. Be it a piece of trash you pick up on a walk, a coworker you compliment, or a problem you are able to solve for someone, find ways to leave the world a little better.

172. Intangible Validation

Push against societal validation.

You are being reminded to make sure your motives for quality of life align with intangible feelings of peace, connection, and harmony instead of the superficial validations society pushes upon you. Take a survey today of what you don't need to spend more energy obtaining.

173. Be Proactive

Control your response.

You can't control what happens around you, but you can control your response to it. Today your angels want you to focus on creating a plan of action in your own life for dealing with incoming challenges. Create a time management structure and organize your work and living space.

174. Limit Distractions

Stay focused on your goals!

Staying focused right now is the message your angels are sending through this number. Limit distractions that keep you from completing what you started. Move to a quiet area, communicate to others that you will be unavailable, and put your phone on airplane mode.

175. Passionate Pursuits

Align your goals to your heart's desire!

Your angels want your life to be as fulfilling as possible. You are being asked to tap in to your passion and pursue projects that reflect it. Take a step back today from something that doesn't align with your strongest feelings.

176. Priority Shift

Establish spiritual intentions.

You may be noticing that the people in your life, the conversations you want to have, and the goals you set are more aligned with your spiritual interests than material ones. Take the cue your angels are sending you and keep going. Create an intention for your spiritual growth! Write it down and say it out loud during the next new moon.

177. Cultivate Calm

Create daily rituals of peace.

Cultivate a routine in which your fears are acknowledged, validated, and then calmed. Your fear and anxiety may not go anywhere, but they don't have to control you. Create space to accommodate them in your daily life without letting them run the show. Implement a ritual of meditation, talks with a professional, or physical activity to ease these emotions.

178. Personal Achievement

You will get what you need!

You are here to do an important job: You are needed in this world to make a change. This number delivers the angelic assurance that you will receive abundance in order to complete your goals. Repeat this mantra: "I welcome the abundance needed to reach my goals."

179. Emotional Intelligence

Pay attention to your intuition.

The feelings that are not sitting right with you need to be acknowledged. They are your direct lines to the divine. Trust that you have the emotional intelligence within to pay these cues the attention they deserve, and shift course appropriately. Where can you listen to your emotions today?

180. Be Clear
State it simply!

Get clear on what you want to receive from the universe. You have to know what you want in order for the universe to give it to you. When you have no plan, the universe will respond with continued confusion. Today, state simply to the universe what it is you want.

181. Intuitive Choices
The right choice will resonate.

The choices you make need to be made intuitively rather than based on what others want from you. Decisions need to resonate within you in order for them to be correct. Take some time away from others today to process a present situation and determine what to do next.

182. Self-Expression
Be intentionally *you*.

You are being asked to become intentional about your forms of self-expression. How you speak, dress, style your room, and even the background on your laptop are all reflections of your unique self. Be intentional today in noticing your expression, and start to own and appreciate it.

183. Represent Yourself
Be true to you!

Your angels want you to ensure that you represent yourself authentically in all you say and do. There are present circumstances in which aligning yourself with the majority opinion isn't reflective of who *you* are. Think about how you can respond differently than those around you.

184. Validation

It's okay to let go.

You are being validated in your intuitive urge to let go of a person or situation at this time. Your angels acknowledge the doubts that may fill you. They give you permission to feel conflicted, sad, or even confused. Consider listing the ways your life could be different without this element present.

185. Positive Change

You create your world!

The challenge now is to take what has happened to you and create something positive. You are creating your reality by demonstrating to the universe how you react to the changes that inevitably occur. Repeat this mantra: "I activate positive change."

186. Trust Yourself

Speak clearly and confidently.

When expressing yourself, your angels want you to trust your instincts and not what others may want to hear from you. Your ability to pick up on what they need is clouding your own voice. Lie down with your hands on your throat chakra. Repeat this mantra: "My voice is strong."

187. Clarity

Know what you want.

You can't get what you want if you don't know what it is. Today, your angels are asking you to state clearly into the universe exactly what it is that you want. Write it on a piece of paper and place it where you can see it and speak it often.

188. Fruitful
Live in gratitude.

Your angels want you to embrace an abundance mindset, where you are appreciative for all you have and live in a state of gratitude. Focus on what you have today, rather than on what you're lacking. Write a list of what you are grateful for right now; there is nothing too small to mention!

189. Heal
You are a lightworker!

You are being called to work on a higher-vibrational frequency. Your angels validate that you have the ability to heal others with your empathic skills. Research ways to aid those who desire spiritual alignment of their own.

190. Transition
Feel your feelings.

There is a significant transition happening in your life presently. Your angels encourage you to find acceptance in what is and closure in what was, while still acknowledging that change can be difficult. Today, allow yourself to feel your emotions freely; write about what you are feeling.

191. New Opportunities
Make a positive change.

When you are excited about new opportunities and people coming your way, better things will arrive. You are being encouraged to focus on the positives in new situations, and look forward to the challenges that will inevitably come with them. Repeat this mantra: "I am ready for positive change."

192. New Normal

Focus inward.

This is a message from your angels that your present circumstances reflect what the "new normal" is for your life. You are being supported as you come to accept what has changed. Turn your focus inward as you find comfort in the one thing that never leaves you: your connection to the divine.

193. Mindset

You are in control!

You are only in charge of how you respond to what is happening around you. You can make the best out of any situation that finds its way to you. Write down this mantra: "I am in control of my responses." Place it where you will see it often.

194. Recognition

Notice your successes.

The road you've traveled has been fraught with challenges. Your angels recognize that it can be hard to see the good things when you are so used to dealing with the hardships. Today, notice the successes and achievements that have come from your dedicated focus.

195. Be Adventurous

Leave the comfort zone behind!

New opportunities will come to you when you foster an adventurous attitude. Your angels encourage you to get far out of your comfort zone today. Lean into the uncertainty by going to that restaurant you've always wondered about, meeting up with the person your friend keeps mentioning, or taking that hot yoga class you've heard so much about.

196. Question Yourself

Take note of your patterns.

You are being directed to take careful notice of your own patterns in your thoughts, feelings, and behaviors. Ask yourself these four questions today and record your answers: What went well today? What went poorly today? What have I learned? How can I improve?

197. Give Energy

Help a worthy cause.

There is a pull within you to give your energy toward the greater good. You are being called to assist with needed change by joining your voice with other like-minded souls. Take up a cause today close to your heart, and think of ways to add your energy to it!

198. Generous Life

Spread love!

Helping others helps your own level of satisfaction in life. Your angels are directing you to spread love and generosity in your daily world. Spend time helping out a person in need, donate whatever you can to others, or participate in a worthy cause.

199. Acceptance

Welcome new beginnings.

Your angels caution you against holding on to things that no longer serve your current season of life. They urge you to accept the reality of the situation and embrace closure so as to welcome new beginnings. Write down something you need to let go of, and burn the paper as a symbol of your release.

200. Good Luck

You make your own fortune in life.

You have been working hard in life. Sometimes it's necessary to expect good things to come out of it, not just more hard work! Your angels want to send you that lucky break, big opportunity, and moment of respite, but you have to believe it's coming. Write down something you would like to manifest and place it in a part of your home where you see it often.

201. Patterns

How you do one thing, you do everything.

What are the small things you do in your daily life that create bigger ripples in your world? Your angels are asking you to take a closer look at your patterns of behavior and ask yourself how they play a role in the bigger picture. Write down a way in which you feel dissatisfied with life, and try to find the pattern underneath it. Reflect on how that pattern shows itself in other places in your life.

202. Problems

The solution is disguised as a problem!

Through the proper perspective, the problem you have right now is actually pushing you toward an authentic solution. Your angels note that you are seeing what does work by sorting through and letting go of what does not. Take a step back and visualize this problem through a broader perspective!

203. Good Friends

Build your support group.

Building a support group of like-minded and loving friends is important for your well-being. Your angels encourage you to spend energy on those who understand what unconditional love is. Make a plan today to reach out to a high-vibing, supportive friend and just have fun!

204. Intangible Treasures

Keep your values close to you.

The values you have are part of you. They are intangible treasures. Your angels want you to honor them in all you do. Keep them at the forefront of your mind by writing them down and placing them where you look often.

205. Cultivating Voice

Hear yourself clearly.

Cultivating an ability to listen to your inner voice is necessary. Your angels are asking you to use meditation, journaling, and reflection to strengthen this ability. When you are able to hear yourself more clearly, the answers to everything can show themselves.

206. Growth Opportunities

Experience humble moments.

There are many relationships and interactions around you that are creating opportunities to learn and grow. Practice humility as you listen with an open mind and see with open eyes what others have to say and show you. Think about how you can incorporate their wisdom into your own life.

207. Make Connections

Look beyond differences!

Your angels are pointing to a conflict in your life with another person. Instead of seeing what is different between you, you are challenged to find the thread of commonality. Brainstorm how to connect via these similarities rather than focus on the differences.

208. Gratitude Everywhere

Challenge yourself to be thankful.

There is always something to be grateful for, no matter how dire the present circumstances may seem. Your angels challenge you to focus on gratitude. Write a list of what you are grateful for today; nothing is too inconsequential to include!

209. Accept Facts

Embrace the reality.

There is a challenge in your life right now that requires acceptance. Your angels acknowledge that you can't change it, so you must accept the reality of it. Write about what you can do now, and what you do not have control over.

210. Faith

Believe in yourself!

The time to take action in your journey is now. Your angels are calling upon your abilities to help others. You are being offered new opportunities to show others their own spiritual pathways in life. Think about a way in which you can help others facilitate their spiritual connections.

211. Assert Conviction

Your faith is needed to make big leaps in life.

Angels are sending you messages, and all you need to do is believe them. Make a list of all the angel numbers, signs, and symbols you've been seeing lately, no matter how small. Meditate on the gratitude you feel for this divine force of love.

212. Honesty

There is power in truth.

Your angels see you building a life, but they call upon you to get honest with yourself about why you are making these choices. Understanding your inner motivations is helpful in living your most blessed life, though it can be uncomfortable to get honest. Spend time in nature today gently thinking about a part of you that you tend to overlook or get distracted from.

213. Self-Doubt

You are capable!

The things coming your way will make you question your own abilities, but your angels want you to know you aren't being sent anything you can't handle. The challenges you are sent have been designed specifically for you, as things you can master along your journey. Repeat this mantra: "I am worthy. I am capable."

214. Give Thanks

Gratitude is your connection to abundance.

Your angels ask you to pause and connect to gratitude. Recognizing what you have is how you create paths to further blessings. What are the things you can sit with and be thankful for today? Create a gratitude list and feel your connection to the divine deepen.

215. Take Charge

You have more power than you know.

Your angels are alerting you to a situation that feels out of control. They remind you that your only control lies in your reactions. In a nature walk today, converse with your angels about what your fears and anxieties are. Feel your angels taking them from you one by one.

216. Treasure

Blessings surround you.

You are surrounded by beauty every moment of your life, and your angels are nudging you to see it! What little things do you experience every day that have been lacking your appreciation? Be very observant today as you create a list of all the blessings you see around you but don't always treasure.

217. Attitude

Keep up the good work.

The effort you've put in and the optimistic vibration you've brought to it have not gone unnoticed by your angels! They applaud your positive attitude in the midst of frustrating times. Reward yourself today in a way that makes you feel self-nurtured. Take a bath, enjoy a special treat, or simply put aside time for yourself to feel calm and relaxed.

218. Gratitude Check

Take inventory of your blessings.

Your angels want to keep sending you gifts of the heart, but they need to know you appreciate those you've already received. Make a gratitude list today that reflects all things you feel particularly called to mention to your angels.

219. Refocus

Look closer at your career goals.

The time to solidify exactly what you want to do in your career is now. If it's to stay where you are, double down on professional development. If it's to switch things up, get serious about the job search. Your angels call on you to take decisive action today.

220. Be Resolute

You have the power within you.

Your angels signal to you that your bravery is seen and applauded. There are those who are benefiting from you right now; your vulnerability and advocacy matter. Repeat this mantra: "I am powerful."

221. Future Outlook

Your past is for you to learn from, not dwell in.

The seasons of your life that are gone don't ask you to linger within them. They inspire you to learn and ready yourself for what's next. Write down what you need to release; then, during the next full moon, burn or bury the paper and feel yourself being set free!

222. Trust Fall

Your angels ask you to trust your place in life right now.

You are in the right place at the right time. Take a look around and enjoy the moment. Everything is where it's supposed to be.

223. Calm Down

It's okay to take breaks.

Your angels are alerting you to your anxiety. They want you to take inventory of what you can let go of so as to avoid overdoing things. Work on your breathing today as a way to center yourself. Take three deep, cleansing breaths and repeat this mantra: "I am peaceful. I am safe."

224. Fundamentals

Secure your life.

As you think of what you are building in your life today, your angels guide you to think of something you've taken for granted. The foundational people, places, and opportunities in your life need your attention. Think of something you've overlooked in your life and give it your energy today.

225. Flexible Mind

Adaptability is key.

Accepting the changes around you is what your angels are calling on you to do. Adaptability will create pathways in your life leading to your soul's purpose. Let something go today that you've tried to resist or control. In meditation today, ask your angels to help you surrender to what comes next.

226. The Heart

You embody love.

To attract love, you must emulate love. Loving yourself is how you create relationships with others that replicate the same love. Lie in meditation today with your hands over your heart chakra. Repeat this mantra: "I am love."

227. Befriend Fear

You are stronger than your fears.

Fear is not an indication of success or failure; it just exists within us. As you manifest your goals and dreams, take into consideration where fear creeps in and limits you. It's not going anywhere, so it's time to make friends with your fear! Write a letter to your fear; befriend it and reassure it that you are okay.

228. Recognize Value

Building a life relies on gratitude for what you already have.

Hold something in your heart that is dear to you. Visualize it and feel the appreciation you have for it fill your soul. Feel the uplifting emotions flow through you. Feel the overflowing of love that comes from connecting to divine gratitude.

229. Hold On

Do not let go of your dream right before it arrives!

The road has been long, and your angels acknowledge that you are tired. But quitting now is not an option. Take a break today so as to motivate yourself to keep going tomorrow. Bask in the sun, walk barefoot in nature, or take a well-deserved nap all in the name of self-care.

230. Self-Development

Work on a weakness.

Your angels want you to pinpoint a skill or activity you know could be enhanced in your life. Now make a plan to develop it! Take twenty minutes today to work on that skill you always wanted to improve upon.

231. Patience

Find peace in the present moment.

Your angels present to you an opportunity to practice patience. Step away from technology, people, and commitments today and feel the quiet of the present moment. Sip coffee while watching the birds, put your bare feet in the grass and note how it feels, and contemplate how nature has its own perfect timeline.

232. Build

This is not impossible, but it is hard work.

The life you want will not come to you overnight. You are building it now with every thought, word, and deed. And your angels ask you to recommit yourself now to your soul's purpose. Write an intention you have and at the next new moon, state it out loud under the stars.

233. Gratitude Rituals

Be thankful in everyday life.

Your angels call upon you to insert a prayer of gratitude into every mundane act you do today. Washing dishes, folding laundry, or driving your car are all chances to contemplate the things you are thankful for. Bask in the glow of the blessings you've already received in life!

234. Words Matter

Align your thoughts.

As you travel along your soul's journey, your angels ask you to align your thoughts and words for support. How does what you say match up to what you want? Journal about a moment recently when you said something that opposed what you actually wanted.

235. Thank You

Gratitude is a great attitude.

There is a person in your life who needs to hear the gratitude you have for them in your heart. Think of someone whom you count on but rarely take the time to effusively thank. Do this today in a heartfelt and genuine way!

236. Make Change

The thing you dislike—do something about it!

Avoidance doesn't work anymore. Your angels acknowledge that you will have to change the thing in your life that is creating a problem presently. Take the first step toward diminishing this issue in your life by creating a plan of direct action.

237. Take Responsibility

Reflect growth in your choices.

Your angels want you to see things around you that you've contributed to and take ownership of them. Being accountable is part of creating an aligned existence with your soul plan. What can you be responsible for that you've been ignoring lately?

238. Give Blessings

Remember those who helped you.

The person who helped you when you had no one: Remember them today. If you can reconnect, do so, and share with them your genuine gratitude. If you are not able to do this, pay it forward in some way in their memory.

239. Different Perspective

Take new chances.

Your angels note that in everything that has changed and left, there is room for new growth. Look at something differently! Consider something with an altered perspective and see how it can now benefit you.

240. Little Things

Pay attention to the things that often go unnoticed.

There are many little things your angels don't want you to dismiss. Instead, look at them with wonder and awe, and, most importantly, with gratitude. There is nothing too small for you not to appreciate today! Create a gratitude list as you go about your day.

241. Construct

Creating takes effort.

Doors will open for you, but behind them will be hard work. Your angels ask you to prepare yourself for this, starting today. Repeat this mantra: "I am comfortable being uncomfortable when I am creating the life I want!"

242. Power

You are very capable.

Being aware of the power of your thoughts and words is necessary today. Your angels want you to know that your mental state reflects in every relationship, opportunity, and environment you end up in. Be the observer of all your thoughts and self-talk today!

243. Impressive Views

Feel thankful.

Your angels want you to be meticulous in your gratitude today. Notice everything in your life and give thanks for it. As you work on your gratitude list, note the lessons, the gifts, and the fruits of your past sacrifices that are now part of your daily life!

244. An Angel
Be the giver!

Giving back in a way you were given to is what your angels ask of you today. When you were in need of divine intervention, your angels provided for you. Today, be a vehicle for your angels to help another. Think of a place or person you can give some of your time to today.

245. Almost There
Push through to the end!

Navigating current life circumstances can feel like an uphill battle. Your angels urge you to push through. They fill you with strength and purpose, determination and drive. Several times today repeat this mantra: "I am filled with divine strength."

246. Paused
Speak in gratitude.

Your angels are validating that certain aspects of your life feel stagnant. The easiest and most powerful way to get things moving again is through gratitude. Today, as you go about your routine, be thankful for every little thing that is moving and working in your favor. Focus on that, and the rest will soon follow!

247. Embrace Lessons
Take advantage of opportunities to learn.

The things that present themselves as problems are actually opportunities for you to demonstrate your abilities to overcome. Your angels want you to tackle a present obstacle in a way that is not only efficient, but is also reflective and embracing of the lessons it offers you.

248. Return Favors

Your angels do not work alone!

Oftentimes your angels send someone in your life to channel their power through helpful acts. Think of someone who has selflessly been there for you recently. Find a meaningful way to connect with them that reflects the gratitude you have in your heart.

249. Reflect

Express gratitude for lessons learned.

The endings that are upon you can have you feeling mournful. But your angels ask you to reflect in gratitude, giving thanks for lessons learned. Write something down today that you are conflicted about letting go. Bury or burn the paper and say a prayer of thanks as you watch it disappear.

250. Show Regard

Make someone's day.

The people in your life in need of appreciation are being pointed out by your angels. Demonstrate gratitude and love to them in words and gestures! Choose someone in your life today whom you can make feel special.

251. Listen

Be open to hearing good advice.

When you hear good advice, you'll hear it more than once, and from multiple sources. Your angels are giving you a message, channeling it through the people and places around you. Listen carefully today to all messages, and find the common link. There is good advice within them.

252. Skill Master

Your lessons matter.

The skill you are currently perfecting is the vehicle by which your life is transported. The lessons you learn today create the realities of tomorrow. Visualize what your life will look like when you have mastered this skill and are using it successfully in everyday life.

253. Confidence

You trust yourself!

If you look at where you are now versus where you have been, you will see how much you've grown in trusting yourself. This is exactly what your angels are asking you to spend time reflecting on today. Write a journal entry about a particular lesson you've learned regarding confidence.

254. Past

Appreciate the lessons you've learned!

The life you live today would not have been possible if you hadn't learned from the lessons of the past. Your angels are proud of the work you've put in for personal growth and responsibility. Write a list of what you are grateful for today that resulted from lessons of the past.

255. New Choices

Changes are indicators.

The changes that are coming bring new decisions for you to make. Your angels encourage you to greet these as signs that your intentions are coming to be. Repeat this mantra: "I know what choices to make when challenges come my way."

256. Optimism

Focus on the good.

Your angels want you to be optimistic about what is to come. Although it's important to acknowledge both the good and the bad in life, your angels want you to spend more time focusing on the good today. As the day goes on, make a list of all the wonderful things you see and experience, no matter how small.

257. Humility

You heard the truth!

The blessings you have today are because you were humble enough to hear the truth yesterday. Write a letter to your past self and express your gratitude and thanks for the version of you that wasn't too proud to listen—even when what you had to hear was difficult.

258. Building Dreams

Take one moment at a time!

The things you do today are part of a bigger picture. Your angels encourage you to treat each moment today as a precious building block of a much larger structure. Draw, write, or contemplate as you visualize what it will all look like when it's completed.

259. Mindfulness

Be present.

Divine wisdom will come when you are present in your daily life. Your angels remind you to be mindful of your thoughts, feelings, and actions today. They ask you to observe these things in real time. To stay present through the day, repeat this mantra: "I am here, I am now, I am mindful."

260. Respect

Foster self-respect, and the world will treat you better!

Your angels want you to respect yourself the way you respect others. Think of a place in your life presently where you don't feel respected. What can you do to limit your personal responses that continue to partake in this energy?

261. Compromise

Meet someone halfway.

Someone you love needs you to meet them halfway. Your angels suggest that you do that! Brainstorm creative solutions to compromise with this person. Show them you care by bringing them into the discussion.

262. You're Flourishing

Value opportunities to learn.

The insights that are coming into your life wouldn't exist without the change that prompted them. You have an opportunity to grow and learn! Write about a lesson you are currently learning and how you feel it will impact your overall personal growth.

263. High Expectations

The more you do, the more you get!

Because you have demonstrated your reliability to others, more opportunities are coming your way. The higher expectations people have of you, the more you can achieve, but you may also feel fear of failure more acutely. Frequently repeat this mantra: "I am capable."

264. Revisit

Update your intentions!

It's time to revisit the intentions you've set in the past. They need an update. Your world has shifted since you made them, and it's time to create new and improved intentions that reflect your present reality. Write them down, and during the next new moon speak them out loud.

265. Self-Progress

Embrace the journey of you!

There is no end point, only a journey. Your angels want you to dedicate yourself to continuous self-improvement in this lifetime. Take today to think about what areas of your life you can work on, and make a plan to do so.

266. Choose You

Make yourself happy.

You are being guided to make your happiness a priority today. Take control over your joy by actively choosing yourself in this moment. Listen to your favorite music, express yourself creatively, or perform an act of kindness!

267. Realization

It's your story.

The perspective from which you see what has happened to you needs to be reframed. Instead of falling into a mindset of victimization, look at how a relevant moment, situation, or interaction has sparked a monumental realization. Today think of a past situation where you were made aware of, educated by, or enlightened by something or someone that hurt you.

268. New Priorities

Regain control over your life!

There are people and situations in your life that no longer serve you, yet you still cling to them. Your angels want you to see this and reprioritize. Ask yourself where you are being influenced negatively, and take action to enact more control.

269. Research

Prepare your response.

A lot of what is happening around you cannot be stopped or controlled, but your angels remind you that you do have power over your understanding of these things. Today, get as informed as you can be about what is presently occurring. Be prepared for how you will respond.

270. Be Alert

Messages are everywhere!

As you are building your life, the messages from your angels are rapid and strong. Take time today to look around and notice what stands out to you. Your angels speak in repetition, so keep that in mind when any signs and symbols capture your interest.

271. Gratitude Attitude

Focus on the positive takeaways.

Today, an attitude of gratitude will serve you best. The present circumstances are easy to approach with negativity, but your angels challenge you to do the opposite. Write about what you can do to reflect thankfulness for the lessons learned and the experiences had.

272. Friendship

It's quality over quantity.

As you build your life around your goals and intentions, you may notice that you don't need as many surface-level relationships as you once did. Your higher self seeks quality over quantity in friendships. Make plans to spend time with a friend today who you feel connected to on a deeper level.

273. Work Smart

Work smarter, not harder!

The work you are doing can be done more efficiently. Use your skills and resources to find creative ways to lighten your load. Brainstorm some ways you can work smarter, not harder.

274. Maintain Focus

Take breaks, but don't quit.

Your angels want you to stay focused, but they understand that it can be difficult to maintain the energy you need to complete the tasks at hand. Take a break here and there today, but create a schedule to get back to work afterward!

275. Support Others

Help yourself by helping someone else.

A surefire way to get your dreams fulfilled is to help others with their dreams. Feel the passion someone has for a dream of their own, and take part in assisting them! Their win is your win too, and that energy facilitates your own goals moving forward.

276. Reevaluating
New ideas shape your life.

Your angels are noticing that you have been shifting, refocusing, and developing your belief system to coincide more authentically with your higher self. Create an intention for your life to further align your goals with your spiritual growth. Say it out loud during the next new moon!

277. Basics
Don't self-destruct!

The anxiety and fear you experience needs to be addressed with love, not destruction. Self-harming habits used to quell your disquieted emotions are not helpful in the long term. Implement healthy habits such as a good night's rest, a wholesome diet, and regular walks.

278. Share Victories
Give credit where it's due.

When you reach a goal, your angels want you to remember who helped you along the way. You can claim a win and still give credit to the ones who assisted and supported you. Share your gratitude for someone who contributed to your personal successes.

279. Synchronicity
Look for signs!

Things that keep happening are connected even if they don't seem to be! When you see patterns in your life, consider that they may be signals from your angels. Today, ask for follow-up signs and remember that angels speak with lots of repetition.

280. Visualize Emotion
Feel it!

Your desired goal will be more than just a reality you see and live in, it's one you will have deep emotions about as well! Today, visualize what you will feel emotionally when you have what you want. Be specific with your emotional visualization and feel it as if it already exists.

281. Demonstrate Trust
Build trust in your intuition.

Your angels want you to build trust in your natural connection to self and the divine. You are being asked to demonstrate trust in yourself by way of making a choice that feels good to you rather than simply looking good to others. Think of where this is applicable today.

282. Feel Good
Shift the expectations.

It doesn't matter if you are good at something; what matters is how you feel doing it. Your angels invite you to begin something new, and focus on the feelings during it rather than the results and what others may view as desirable. Do something new today, and whether you succeed or fail, note how you feel.

283. Embrace Individuality
You are a unique soul who has important work to do.

There are those around you who would rather see you mirror their own ideals and dreams, but you have a unique journey you must go on! Today, explore who or what is holding you back from doing what you want to do.

284. It's Inevitable

Welcome acceptance.

There is an inevitable outcome to what you are presently dealing with in your life. Your angels call on you to welcome it with acceptance. Peace will fill you when you let go of the need to control what is happening. Repeat this mantra: "I feel peace."

285. Prioritize

Create direction.

Your angels want you to sort out what makes you happy in your life. Such a basic question has become deprioritized in your busy life. Today, spend time thinking about your dreams, what and who makes you happy, and create direction out of your answers.

286. Be True

Maintain your perspective.

You are being reminded to form your own judgments about the present situation. There are others around you who have unique perspectives on the subject, but it is important to maintain your own. Journal about how you feel presently and note how others can affect you.

287. Speak Gratitude

Act "as if."

It is easier for you to get what you desire if you already respond in gratitude for it. Instead of stating, "I want..." say, "I am grateful for..." Act as if you already have what it is you want, and the power of manifesting will intensify!

288. Friendships Matter

Create meaningful connections.

You have people around you who can lift you up, as well as those who can do the opposite. It is not selfish to spend more time and energy on the positive people in your life. Make plans to spend time with a person who lifts you up, fosters personal growth, and supports you!

289. Vocation

Connect with others.

Your angels acknowledge that you feel compelled to help or heal people around you. They encourage you to follow this vocation and reach out to others who do the same. Join a like-minded community of people or reach out to someone you can converse with about this pull to help others.

290. Past Gifts

Focus on the lessons learned.

It will be easier to let go of the past when you focus not on what you've lost but on what you've gained. Write a list of what you've learned from significant people and events in your life. Feel gratitude for what was and what stays with you today.

291. Set Precedent

Eliminate distractions.

There is a calling for you to prioritize what it is you want. There are many distractions around you presently, and the challenge is to keep your mind set on what you actually want. Eliminate distractions today by postponing or declining anything that isn't essential.

292. Channel Anxiety
Create positive distractions.

The anxiety and grief you are experiencing can be overwhelming. Your angels acknowledge this. They urge you to channel these into a positive distraction. Volunteer some time, reorganize a closet, or take up a new physical activity such as walking or jogging.

293. Framework
Look where the good outweighs the bad.

You are being asked to restructure your mental framework to accommodate the new challenges that seek you out. Focus on the positives in every situation in order to see how they make you a stronger person.

294. Celebrate Triumphs
Everyday accomplishments matter!

In order to receive success, you must celebrate the everyday versions of it. Take time to focus on your successes today, no matter how small you may perceive them to be. Congratulate yourself on organizing your garage, making an insightful observation at work, or putting together a nice outfit for yourself.

295. Enjoy Life
Make the everyday fun.

Your life is here to be enjoyed, not endured! You are asked to make some fun out of the everyday life you live. Seek out something that interests you and prioritize it. Start a new book, try out a different hairstyle, or make a plan to visit a restaurant you've been wondering about.

296. Open Mind

Find the counterargument.

Your angels ask you to pick up a book, read an article, or engage with a counterargument to your existing way of thinking. Open your mind to new perspectives, if for no other reason than to learn from them.

297. Create Space

Inform others of the situation.

There is information that needs to be given to those around you. Your angels are calling on you to organize a space in which to inform people of what is presently happening. Create a focused goal, and get to work creating pathways for educating others.

298. Generosity

You are being asked to give of yourself on behalf of another person.

The generous spirit of someone in your life needs to be honored. Your angels encourage you to make a small donation of money, time, or items in the name of a person who has done good things selflessly for you and others.

299. Thrive

Evolve your thinking!

You are given the go-ahead to embrace new ways of thinking. Your angels remind you that evolving your thoughts, ideals, and values is a sign of personal growth. Journal about how a view you had in the past has changed drastically over time and why.

300. Divine Connection

The mind, body, and spirit unite.

Your angels acknowledge that you have an intense connection to the divine right now! The unity of your mind, body, and spirit creates a conduit for spirit messages. Lie in meditation today with your hands on your third eye chakra (the center of the forehead). Repeat this mantra: "I trust in my abilities."

301. Renew Love

A relationship needs attention.

Your angels are signaling that an important relationship in your life needs renewal and attention. We often hurt the ones we love the most, and you are being called to recognize that. Who in your life could use a little tender loving care? Think of one way you can show a person you love that they are still as special to you as the day you first met them.

302. Ask

Angels speak through others.

Asking for support in solving a problem is highly encouraged by your angels at this time. The unique perspectives of others will assist you in making a good decision for yourself. Ask a trustworthy person in your life for their input into what is troubling you.

303. Be Peace

Set your mind right.

Your mindset is of the utmost importance right now. Your angels implore you to get on a frequency of peace and tranquility. You are allowed to remove yourself from the presence of people or situations that detract from this. Repeat this mantra: "I am peace." Today, take time for *you*.

304. Be United

Define your values.

A present circumstance is challenging a belief or value you hold dear. Become more united with your values by writing them down in your own words and explaining what they uniquely mean to you. Do this today, focusing on a value that feels challenged by the outside world.

305. Self-Care Day

Pamper your inner voice!

Pampering yourself a little will strengthen your ability to listen to and trust your inner voice. When you give yourself the care and love you deserve, your voice within becomes more confident in speaking out. Take a self-care day and be patient with your intuitive thoughts as they come to you.

306. Resemblance

Do not compare yourself with others.

Your angels are telling you that comparison leads to endless unhappiness. Instead, focus inward on your personal growth. Be mindful of the habits of thought that lead you to compare. When your mind veers into negative comparison, replace the thought with encouragement to grow within.

307. Have Fun

Don't self-isolate!

Self-isolation is not the answer to what you are currently undergoing. Your angels urge you to make meaningful and fun connections with people whom you trust to support you. Make a plan today to spend time with someone who makes you remember how to feel good.

308. Self-Aware Friends

Meet supportive people.

You are called to surround yourself with people who are self-aware and committed to their own personal growth. Allow them to move you forward and cheer you on. Say yes to a gathering or community get-together in which you can meet some supportive people who inspire you.

309. Essentials

Make life easier where you can.

Things will pick up soon in your life. Today, make a list of all the things that need to be done. Make appointments for physical and mental well-being care, get your car's oil changed, and clean out a closet. Take control where you can before things get too busy.

310. Transfer Energy

Giving is receiving.

Your angels are asking you to channel the divine and give back to those in need. Your own gift comes when you give to others. Take inventory of a few people in your life who may need more than they feel comfortable asking for, and do something special for them.

311. Rewards

All your hard work has been noticed.

The efforts you've been putting into your life are not unnoticed by your angels. The work you've done that has seemingly gone unrecognized by others will now be rewarded in a way you need it most! Visualize yourself accepting the reward with gratitude and love in your heart.

312. Help Yourself

Knowledge is power!

Your angels are asking you to educate yourself to bring about success. This could be through a class, a workshop, or a certification. List a goal you have and all the steps you need to take to achieve it.

313. Decide Today

Make a choice to move forward.

The decision you've been going back and forth about needs to be decided on. Your angels are saying that you already know the answer, but also that the non-answer is controlling you. Quietly meditate on what you want your life to look like after this choice has been made; visualize the freedom you feel having made it.

314. Plan It

Organize your next steps.

Your angels are telling you to pause and focus so as to make correct choices moving forward. What are your goals? And what is your current plan for meeting them? Seeing this number is a message to review that plan today!

315. Declutter Life

Create mental space.

Your state of mind is a direct reflection of your physical space. Your angels are signaling to you that work needs to be done here. Declutter your space to declutter your mind. Tackle a closet, desk, or garage today. Recycle or give away what you can!

316. Lend Aid

Helping hands make light work!

Your angels ask you to volunteer your time to a project today. The energy you give toward a selfless act will be returned to you three-fold. Think of a person or place that needs your assistance, and plan some time to help out.

317. You're Heard

Your prayers are answered.

Your angels want you to know that they see you and are with you all the time, holding you in times of happiness and struggle. They are sending you a sign to let you know they hear you. Look for it, and send thanks when you see it.

318. Expansion

Open spaces in your life for abundance to enter!

You can't deliver more to a cluttered mindset. Your angels are asking you to tackle some issues in your life that create imbalance. Plan a time to have a heartfelt conversation today with someone—a friend, counselor, or other trusted person—in a space where you feel heard.

319. Relationships

Bring forth new love.

If you are in a relationship, this number is a signal to do something to reinforce the bond between you. If you are single, this is prime time to bring forth new love! Lie in meditation as you visualize the white light of the divine shining on your heart chakra, clearing out any debris that blocks these loving energies from coming to you.

320. See Blessings

Ask your angels for direction.

Your angels know that life has been chaotic, and because of that, it's been hard to see your present blessings. Use aromatherapy today to open your senses to the awareness of your highest self. Use a diffuser, light a candle, or smell essential oils to connect to the present moment.

321. Boundaries

It's okay to set limits.

There are those who take too much, and your angels are reminding you that you don't have to let them. It's important to say no to what harms you. Think of a boundary you can set in place today, then put it into motion.

322. Seek Assistance

You are in need of aid.

Your angels see that you've been trying to do it all on your own. They want to give you support in the form of helping hands around you. Ask a friend or a loved one for their help, gratefully receive it, and feel the unconditional love of the divine channel through them.

323. Natural Intelligence

You have a gift of the mind.

You are naturally intelligent, and your angels remind you of this so as to give you confidence and perspective as you move forward out of your present comfort zones. Repeat this mantra: "I am confident and capable."

324. Embrace Harmony

The different versions of you need attention.

You are many different people in many different contexts. Your angels call on you to notice how your work life, your home life, and your spiritual life need a common bond to ensure they are balanced. To establish this connection, repeat this mantra: "I align with my truth"

325. Heart Pains

Grief is accompanying you.

Your angels surround you, hold you, and support you. They are with you during this time when you feel lonely or lost. Speak out loud to your angels today, pen a letter to them about your feelings, and feel them holding space for you.

326. Potential

You are already complete.

Your highest potential lives within you. You aren't searching for it outside yourself but rather are uncovering it within. Lie in meditation with your hands over your root chakra (the base of the spine). Repeat this mantra: "I already am."

327. Appreciation

People will know your name.

This number signifies that people you don't know already know you! Your angels want you to get comfortable being seen. Visualize yourself with a bubble of white, protective light around you. Know that this bubble keeps you safe from anything you don't want infiltrating your boundaries.

328. Be Here

The present moment calls you.

Your angels are asking you to be present. Spend time away from technology today. Allow yourself to be focused without distractions on your own thoughts and emotions. Journal about how it feels in this moment to be completely in the present; be sure to record all your feelings without judgment.

329. Prioritize Friendship

Make time for healthy bonds in your life.

Your angels remind you to take time today to fortify a friendship. Reconnect with an old friend or take the initiative with a new friend. Make a plan for an outing, share a story about yourself, and laugh together as you strengthen the bond.

330. You're Seen

Your actions have been noted!

You've taken care of some things in your life that needed working on. Your angels take note and give praise. Sit in the comfort of knowing you are creating a life of balance in every positive action you take. Contemplate all the unseen forces that have supported you.

331. Request

Solidify what you are asking for.

Your prayers are being heard, but your angels want you to streamline them. Organize exactly what you want and reflect on the best ways to ask for it. In a journal, form a complete request that succinctly asks for what you want in life.

332. Angel Connections

Create a relationship with your angels.

Your angels invite you to speak to them freely. Hold a conversation in nature, or pen a letter to them. Ask them to send you a sign that is uniquely between you and them. Believe it when you see it!

333. Equilibrium

Nurture the mind, body, and spirit connection.

Get some meditation going, embark on a workout routine, and finally start that vision board you've been procrastinating on. Your angels want you to look at the areas of your life that are not fully rounded out, and self-correct.

334. Brave

Courageously ask for what you want.

It's brave to want something. You are being called to spend energy asking for what you want. Create a vision board today, using images and words to detail the future you are looking forward to.

335. Challenge

Your angels gift you with fortitude.

The current moment is presenting conflict. Your angels remind you that you have the strength to get through this. Lie in meditation with your hands on your root chakra (the base of the spine) and repeat this mantra: "I am strong."

336. Assistance

Just ask.

To get assistance, you have to ask for it, and also give it. Your angels encourage you to ask for help, and when the tables turn at some point, pay it forward and *be* the help. Write down what it is that you need without shame, and know it will come to you in divine timing.

337. Conviction

Demonstrate your belief.

Your angels want you to let go of the fear that all you've received will disappear. The blessings you have are because you worked hard and aligned your thoughts to what you desire! Show your faith today by helping another person with their own belief. Encourage a friend or loved one to believe that there is unconditional love surrounding them always.

338. Channel Abundance

You are blessed.

Your angels have good news for you today. Abundance flows to you; prepare yourself to receive it. Lie in meditation today and repeat this mantra: "I am grateful for the blessings that come and look forward to abundance coming my way."

339. Speak Up

Say what's on your mind.

Your angels say it's your turn to lead others. They want you to work on the confidence to do this, and use your voice to turn others to the light. Lie with your hands on your throat chakra and repeat this mantra: "My voice is strong; my voice is steady; I speak my truth."

340. Be Bold
Trust self and spirit.

Your angels want you to fall back on your higher power and know that in doing so, you are building your inner strength. Create time for a meditation today in which you go within, practice deep breathing, and feel yourself remaining calm and peaceful no matter what the world is doing outside.

341. Companionship
Love helps you!

Your angels want to give you a supporting partner. If you are single, start noticing the new people entering your life. If you are in a relationship, notice where it's been strengthened lately. Lie in meditation with your hands over your heart chakra and repeat this mantra: "I am loved."

342. Urgent
Take a closer look!

There is something recently dismissed and disregarded that needs your attention. Your angels want you to know that this is important, and taking a closer look will have benefits to you beyond this present moment. Reflect on what you've neglected to take seriously lately, and circle back around to do so.

343. Wiggle Room
Find the room for improvement.

Feel around today in your soul, and ask yourself where you have a little bit of defocused energy. The wiggle room of your thoughts, actions, and words is under a microscope today. Contemplate in solitude today, asking yourself, "Where is there room for improvement?"

344. Create Bonds

Make a friend!

Human connection is important, and your angels are asking you to bond with another person. Make a new friend or reconnect with an old one. Have a nice time laughing, feeling joyful, and soul connecting.

345. Baby Steps

Little by little it will get done.

The overwhelm you feel is not unnoticed by your angels. They ask you to reconfigure your perspective, and instead of focusing on the big picture, look at the immediate next step. Organize your thoughts on paper and write down what your upcoming baby steps will be in the forthcoming days.

346. Skipping Steps

Details are important!

You are moving at a faster speed than most lately, and your angels are reminding you to make sure you aren't skipping any necessary steps. Circle back today to a recent situation and make absolutely sure you did not miss any details or processes that could cause an issue later.

347. Health

Take care of your health.

There is an urging from your angels to take seriously a health matter that you have let fall by the wayside. How you treat your body is important: It shows self-love and care. Make a doctor's appointment or address the concern you've been putting off.

348. Neglect

Balance creates harmony.

Your angels see that you neglect certain things that are presently causing imbalance. Acknowledge this lapse in harmony and find a way to address it today. Start with a list of the places in your life you know could use more attention.

350. Harmonious

Create a balance of love!

There is some facet of love in your life that is feeling off-kilter. Make sure you are giving equal attention to self-love, familial love, and romantic love. Choose an area that feels weak and work on it today.

349. Habits

Detoxify your life.

Your angels are telling you that the thing that causes you stress and anxiety, yet also provides a sort of comfort, needs to go. It's hard to let this person, object, or situation go, but you have the support of the divine in doing so. Prepare yourself: This will be a challenge, but you are up for it.

351. Vantage Point

Try a different angle.

The goals and dreams you have need some new life injected into them. Your angels ask you to switch up your perspective and try things from a different angle. If something isn't working, let the method go, but not the goal itself. Brainstorm today a different way to get to the same result.

352. Well-Rounded

Mind, body, and spirit intertwine.

As you are thinking about growth, your angels ask you to focus on the mind, body, and spirit connection as a whole. Contemplate how you can grow one part of yourself and bring the other two into it as well.

353. Work It

Find physical strength.

Your angels want you to demonstrate inner strength and discipline by mirroring it in your physical form. Do a challenging exercise today and show yourself what you're made of! If there are skills you need to develop, take note—and get to it.

354. Self-Tending

Look to where you need healing.

One area of your life needs some tending to. Your angels are asking you to reconfigure your mind, body, and spirit connection today and see what area needs growth. Pick up a self-help book, listen to a new podcast, ramp up a workout, or consider talking to a professional. You are worth this!

355. Genuine Life

Make mindful choices.

The way your life is moving forward is presenting many opportunities for you to make choices that represent your authentic self. Be very mindful today of how your words, actions, and patterns reflect who you authentically are.

356. Vibe Check
Notice the toxic!

Your angels want you to thoroughly vibe-check the people in your close circles. Spending time with low-vibrational energy has a negative effect on your own ability to manifest your best life. Consider a few key people in your life and note carefully how you feel before you spend time with them versus after.

357. Divine Knowing
The truth leads you home.

You can hear difficult things, and your angels applaud you for that. The truth can be upsetting, but accepting it leads to an authentic life. What feels like a backward step is actually a fast track to the future. Repeat this mantra: "I am open to divine wisdom."

358. Stress
Work it out.

Things appear to be moving fast, and your angels want you to work on your emotional response to that. They encourage you to get out and be active today as a way to process the challenges you are undergoing and relieve stress.

359. Discipline
Practice self-control.

Your angels are asking you to demonstrate self-control. Your discipline will become stronger the more you use it. Take a step today to start or stop things based on what you know to be difficult yet necessary for your growth.

360. Prosperous Growth
Learn from life.

There is much to be learned from your current situation, and your angels want you to take this opportunity to do just that. Journal about the lessons you are coming up against now, and how you can utilize them so as to foster a prosperous future.

361. Helping Hands
Be the support another person needs!

There is someone in your life who could use a helping hand but may be too shy or proud to ask for it. Chip in and get to work; make sure they know you want to do this. Tell them that you consider it a privilege and a joy that they allow you to help.

362. Maintain Contact
Be supported by friends.

The people in your life who remain constant are there for you to support you as you undergo the present changes in your life. Make a plan today to connect with someone who is a constant in your world.

363. Strong Relationships
You are dependable.

Your relationships are beginning to strengthen and deepen as a result of your focus on self. You have demonstrated a feeling of stability and reliability to others in your circle. Your angels are applauding you for the journey you've been on to get here. Take in angelic love today, spending time in nature absorbing it.

364. Practice It

Put action behind your intentions.

The intentions you have set need some action behind them. Revisit your intentions and choose one to work on today. Put forth a valiant effort to show the universe and yourself that you are serious about self-growth!

365. Self-Focus

Observe your thoughts.

Your angels remind you that you only have control over your own process of thinking and responding. Focusing on what you can control as opposed to what you cannot is essential. Create a list of what things within your control you would like to focus on in your meditations this week.

366. Nothing Personal

You can only control yourself.

The people and situations around you that affect you are not about you. Your angels remind you that you can't control how others act, but you can control your response to their actions. Journal about how a recent situation feels personal and deep-dive into why it feels that way.

367. Physical Sensations

Be present with your body.

You are asked to get in touch with your body today. The physical sensations you experience can bring you into the present moment. Focus on deep breathing, and as you do so, you will see the changes that bring you toward self-awareness and focus.

368. Utility

The less you have, the freer your mind can be.

Your angels encourage you to add value to your life by tossing some things away. This could be a literal clearing out of your garage and closets, or a metaphorical clearing out of people and situations that are cluttering your connection to self and spirit.

369. Reduce Stress

Revive your mind, body, and spirit!

Your mind, body, and spirit need to decompress. Your angels are alerting you that your stress levels are at an all-time high. Do something that relaxes you today—take a technology break, read a book, or take a contemplative walk in nature.

370. Spirit Journal

Tune in to angel communication.

Your angels want to fortify their connection with you. Get a journal and at the beginning of each week write about what you're grateful for, as well as what you need your angels' assistance with. Look for synchronicity throughout the week and update your journal accordingly.

371. Faithful Leaps

You need a reprieve.

The thing you are worrying about isn't getting any better for all that focused anxiety. Your angels want you to take a respite from this type of thinking and instead trust that you'll know what to do when the situation becomes real. Repeat this mantra: "I have faith it will go as it should."

372. Recharge

Tune out others' energies.

You can absorb the energy around you more easily than others, so you need to take time to recharge. The thoughts and feelings others give out are constantly being picked up by you. Take time alone today to daydream, journal, or enjoy a creative pursuit.

373. Supported Strength

Receive help from others.

Your angels remind you that it's not weak to ask for support when you need it. You are being called to receive the gifts that others have to give to you in the form of their time, love, and energy. Ask for help today from someone who is in a position to give aid!

374. Health First

Take care of your body.

Your body needs some attention. Your angels are reminding you not to ignore your core needs as you push yourself through this challenging time. Incorporate more leafy greens, hydrate often, and get your best night's rest.

375. Modify

Give your mind, body, and spirit attention.

There are modifications needed in your mind, body, and spirit today. Your angels alert you to some habits that will cause self-destruction and depletion in the long term. Reflect on where you could fortify your lifestyle with professional help, healthier foods, or focused spiritual practice.

376. Heartstrings
**Shifts occur when
growth happens.**

Not everyone around you is going to be able to resonate with your spiritual awakening. Your angels remind you that this is okay. If those around you cannot respect your newfound self-awareness, simply wish them light and love and return to your higher self for validation.

377. Talk
Reach out!

You don't have to be alone right now. Talking about your fears will keep them from overwhelming you. Reach out to someone today to share your worries with them. Let them give you love, support, and assistance and know that your angels are working through them.

378. Encourage Others
**Channel your love
through action.**

Encouragement to someone struggling isn't empty words. It is a way to channel positivity, love, and wisdom to someone in a dark time. Your angels want you to reach out to someone in need and give kindness and support.

379. Physical Signs
Your body will talk.

Your body can hold on to messages you aren't listening to. Your angels are asking you to take seriously the feelings in your body right now. Address what is concerning to you medically and also emotionally. Is your body trying to tell you something you haven't been open to?

380. Blessings Everywhere

Focus with gratitude.

Today, show appreciation for the blessings that surround you. Reach out to a friend to thank them for their unconditional love, clean out your closet or car as a sign of respect for what you have, or show yourself some self-care to nourish your soul health!

381. Body Talk

Pay attention to your body!

Your body carries receptors that your angels tap in to. Pay attention to the prickles on the back of your neck, the shivers going down your spine, and the goosebumps appearing. Physical symptoms in the body are responses to spiritual presences around you.

382. Use Feelings

Create via your authentic self.

Being creative when you feel less than motivated is what you are asked to do today. Your angels encourage you to use any emotion you have in order to live life creatively and feel fulfilled. Channel your mood into your work and creative pursuits today. Feel the difference.

383. Friendly Bonds

Instead of conforming, find people who support you!

You are being supported by your angels in finding like-minded people who encourage you on your path. Your angels acknowledge that you may have had some people fall out of your life as you become more authentic. Make a plan with a friend who accepts you for you.

384. Converse

Release your voice.

There is a person in your life you need to have an honest conversation with. Your angels are supporting you in speaking your truth. Today, plan on having this conversation; if this is impossible in person, write a letter to them, even if it will never be delivered.

385. Envision

You need to see your dreams in front of you!

The ability to live life according to your soul's plan requires you to make it a central focus and priority daily. Create a vision board by finding pictures and words that speak to you and forming them into a collage. Place it somewhere you will see it often.

386. Projecting

Process your thoughts.

The will of others is affecting your own judgment. Your angels are cautioning you against someone who is in your inner circle and is projecting their own insecurities, feelings, and wishes upon you. Take time today to process your thoughts and feelings; journal about them honestly.

387. Feel Fabulous

Attract the joy you deserve!

You will align yourself more intensely with your goals and dreams if you feel wonderful inside. Take time today to feel fabulous. Dance to your favorite song, wear your best outfit, or hang out with your most high-vibe friends. Feel joyful for this life you live.

388. TLC
Treat yourself how you want to be treated.

If you want the universe to send you blessings, treat yourself as if you are worthy of them. Spend time today balancing your mind, body, and spirit connection. Look to where you could use a little extra tender loving care in your self-care routine and apply it.

389. Ground Yourself
The earth connects to you!

The care and concern you have for the world you live in and the people and creatures within it are not unnoticed by your angels. They acknowledge that you feel the connectivity of the natural and spiritual world. Ground yourself today by walking barefoot outside and lying in the sun.

390. Press On
Move forward now!

There is a present situation in which you are called to take personal responsibility. You alone are in charge of your future. Ask yourself what you can and cannot control in this situation, and what actions are needed for you to move forward.

391. Imperfection
Be open-minded.

Your angels are cautioning you against the self-destructive tendency to seek perfection. The goals you set need to be achievable and open-minded. Focus on one goal today and visualize the divine taking it into their hands and giving it back to you in perfect form—a form that is of their design, and not necessarily yours.

392. Prioritize Self-Care
The loss you've recently experienced is heavy.

Your angels implore you to take up a self-care routine that is non-negotiable. Make a daily activity list for yourself, and include showering, eating, and sleeping as main goals while you get yourself back on track.

393. Mirror
The past will teach you.

Look to where you've been so far. Reflecting on your past will bring you greater appreciation of your present as well as an idea of what is to come. Write a timeline of major events that have defined you. Reflect on their contributions to where you are today.

394. Visual Reminders
Keep your successes visible!

You need to see your past accomplishments so as to create more of the same in your world. Create some visual reminders of your successes and place them all around you. Frame your diploma, cut out an article you were mentioned in, and hang up that award you won!

395. Hidden Talents
Unearth your skills.

Your angels want you to try to find a new talent that lies dormant within you. Start saying yes to what you previously would have said no to. Take an art class, join an improv group, or allow yourself to try out something you didn't even consider before.

396. Disconnect
Quiet the mind.

There is a need for you to disconnect from your current state of thinking so as to reconnect to your higher self. Journal about the self-awareness you gain from meditation, running, cooking, or some other activity that quiets the mind.

397. Help Others
Use your knowledge to assist.

You have skills that are needed by a greater good. Your angels are calling on you to think creatively about what you know and how that can help a cause move forward. Volunteer your time in some way, help a neighbor, or mentor someone who could benefit from what you know.

398. Gifts
Be thoughtful!

Give a gift today that you know another person will benefit from. You are being asked to generously give something thoughtful to someone who needs it. Think of someone in your life who could use a little pampering, and make a plan to give them some today!

399. Prepare Yourself
Stabilize your inner connection.

Your angels encourage you to steady yourself for the changes to come. They want you to take a look at your mind, body, and spirit connection and focus your energy on stabilizing it. Take a walk in nature or rest without distraction.

400. Have Faith

Your angels hear you.

You are never alone. Your angels have heard your prayers and felt your struggles. They stay with you and remind you that everything has a purpose, even though you may not understand it now. Sit in nature today, and ask your guides to send you love, peace, and signs. Trust what you see and feel when you wholeheartedly ask for these messages.

401. Revive

It's your time to shine!

The light is shining on you now. It's time to take that chance, speak up for yourself, and go for that thing you've been wanting to do but haven't yet. You have a window of opportunity, and your angels are giving you the go-ahead to put some effort forth to get this done. Take a power walk, sing your favorite song, or have a personal dance party. Get the energy moving to take things to the next level!

402. No Rush

Take time to ponder a choice.

There is no rush to solve a problem you are presently dealing with. Feel free to spend a few days pondering and processing the various solutions that come to mind. Create a list of pros and cons, then brainstorm and meditate thoughtfully on what to do next.

403. Prioritize Health

Reignite your goals.

Your angels see the goals you set for your overall well-being and want you to take some action toward those goals today. Go shopping for healthy foods, make time to take a walk, or put aside ten minutes to meditate.

404. Angelic Support
Synchronicity is all around you.

There is a rush of angel activity around you. You are being supported and upheld by the divine. Your prayers are heard, and you are receiving messages and answers everywhere you look. Keep close watch for your angels' signs!

405. Intuition
Study the divine.

The studying of intuition can help you strengthen your own. Learning about the ability to tap in to the divine can help you tap inward as well. Pick up a book on the subject, listen to a podcast, or talk with a like-minded friend.

406. Be Humble
Sit back and learn.

Being humble and teachable is what your angels encourage you to embrace at this time. There are many situations and contexts in which it is best to sit back, learn, and grow. Reflect on how what is happening around you today can teach you useful lessons for tomorrow.

407. Trustworthy
Lend a helping hand!

You have the unique ability to be the person someone else can lean on today. Feel stable and calm because you have confidence in your own inner connection. Lend a listening ear or a helping hand to someone who needs it.

408. Focused Strength

Put yourself in the right places to grow.

You are being directed to focus on your strengths rather than your weaknesses. Acknowledging your limits is important, but focusing on your assets is what gets you ahead. Reflect upon the contexts you find yourself in and examine whether they are conducive to displaying your strengths or not.

409. Missteps Happen

Communicate truthfully in your self-talk.

Taking a look at your missteps along the way is important. Your angels know it's going to sting, but it's necessary to be honest with yourself. Write about a time you made an error and how you can learn from it even today.

410. Help Incoming

It's all coming together now.

The final step in receiving is to have an open mind! Create a list of what you are grateful for in life today as you realize that you have all you need right now. Feel abundantly grateful that more is on its way in divine timing to you.

411. Important Relationships

See the value in those you love.

This number calls you to select one relationship close to you and nurture it in an attentive and loving way. Tell a loved one how much you care for them, appreciate them, and see them in your life. Make time for them as you communicate how important they are to you.

412. Stay Humble

To get where you are going, remember the place you came from.

It's okay to want a different life, but the lessons of the past need to be honored. Try a grounding activity today and ask your angels to give you a feeling of stability. Walking outside barefoot, taking a salt bath, or lying in the sunlight are all wonderful ways to connect to your core self.

413. Financial Freedom

Take back your control.

There is a need for you to look at your finances and get them in order. Organizing, understanding, and budgeting your money are all actions that create pathways for more financial abundance in the future. Spend twenty minutes today tackling one financial predicament you've been ignoring.

414. Powerful Words

Speak to create!

Every word you speak, good or bad, creates your reality. Your angels want you to self-check your outer and inner dialogue. Practice speaking kindly of yourself to others and to yourself. Repeat this mantra: "My words create my reality."

415. Moving

Home is where the heart is.

Your angels are signaling that there may be a move in your future. What can you do now to make the transition run smoothly? Organize your space, declutter your closets, and donate what you don't need as you ready yourself for what's to come.

416. Balance

Get back on track!

There is something amiss in your priorities right now. Your angels encourage you to recognize it and get back on track. Think of where you need to refocus energy. Practice a grounding activity: Walk outside barefoot, lie in the sun, or swim in a body of water.

417. Meditate

Get grounded.

This number is calling you inward. Your angels are suggesting that you may be scattered lately in your thoughts and actions. Meditate today and, as you do, picture a glowing ball of light within you, powering you eternally. This is source energy, and it lives in you!

418. Feared Desires

Trust in the divine.

It's hard to ask for what you want, because if you don't get it, the disappointment can be heavy. Take some time to write a letter to your angels asking them specifically for what you want. Trust that they hear you.

419. Find Assistance

When you ask for what you need, you get support!

There is so much going on right now, and your angels notice you've been trying to do it all yourself. Their support will come in the form of selfless helping hands around you. Look to those who are willing to assist you, and gratefully allow them to do so.

420. Honorable

**Be the energy you
wish to receive.**

There is someone who needs you, and you are in a position to help them. No matter what little *you* think it could do, for this person, it's so much more than you know! Think of someone in your life you need to connect or reconnect with, and do something generous of spirit and heart for them.

421. Comfort

**Feel safe in your present
moment.**

You have assurance from your guides that you are right where you are supposed to be, so rest easy in that faith. Repeat this mantra: "I am safe; I am protected; I am loved."

422. Neglected Foundations

**Look around at what needs
your energy.**

You are being called to focus your manifesting efforts on something foundational in your life that has been taken for granted. Spend time today reflecting on who or what could use some attention from you, and create a plan to give it.

423. Give Yourself

**Demonstrate love as you
help others.**

At some point, there was a helping hand selflessly extended to you that propelled you forward. Now it's your turn to do the same. Think of a person who could use your recommendation, support, or guidance and lend it to them.

424. Thankful

You are grateful for where you have been.

The past is coming up a lot lately, and your angels want you to understand that the lesson here is gratitude. You could not be where you are today without the help of where you were before. Reflect and journal on a lesson of the past that got you to where you are today.

425. Be Courageous

When you find what you want, you'll have to be brave enough to take it!

The things you want require a version of yourself that feels worthy to take them. Your angels ask you to work on that today. Repeat this mantra: "I give thanks for my bravery."

426. Protection

The people who love you protect you.

Your angels want you to be wary of new influences coming into your life from people who don't have your best interests at heart. Trust that the ones who love you speak in truth. Reflect on conflicting forces in your life and ask your angels to give you clarity in what is really going on.

427. In Touch

Connect with the divine.

You have an ability to perceive things that are not of this world. Your angels call on you to connect with this extrasensory skill. Lie in meditation with your index finger tapping on your third eye chakra (the center of the forehead). Repeat this mantra: "I see."

428. Foundational Gratitude

Rebuild your priorities.

The things that never went away, the things that stood still to support you...those are the things to be thankful for today. Your angels want you to look around to the people and places that remained with you during turbulent times and feel gratitude for them. Take time today to demonstrate an act of deep appreciation.

429. Memories

The past stirs up the present.

Your angels acknowledge that a lesson from the past is making its way into your present moment. The emotion it creates in you needs to be addressed. Reflect and journal on what present circumstances are mirroring past ones, and how the lessons of then can assist you with now.

430. Cleanse

Clear your energy.

The energy around you tends to stick on you. Your angels urge you to notice it and clear it. Diffuse essential oils and light a white candle, then visualize white light surrounding you and extending into your space, clearing it of any stale or negative energy. Open a window and a door and know that the energy is moving away from you.

431. Inspect

Look behind you!

You are moving too fast, and the things you rush by are in need of your attention. Look around to what opportunities and relationships are being left behind that aren't solid enough to stand on their own. Make a plan to attend to them.

432. See Yourself

The situation presenting itself in your life right now is not for you.

Your angels remind you that a present circumstance is something that represents a previous version of you, one that you've grown from. Reflect on this situation as a lesson and representation of the past, and journal about how you have changed since last confronting it.

433. Angels Oversee

Ask for help.

You may have been feeling lost in what direction to go in life. Your angels acknowledge this and ask you to put your faith in them. Write down the choices you've been putting off, then ask your angels for divine guidance in how to proceed.

434. Pillars

Be a stable force in an unstable world.

Change is inevitable, but what remains constant is your response to it. Your angels call on you to differentiate what you can control from what you cannot. Brainstorm some ways you can remain in control with your words and actions in times like these.

435. Goodbye

The chapter has ended.

The present moment is one that requires you to say goodbye. It's okay to be sad, to mourn what was. Your angels hold you at this time. Repeat this mantra: "I allow myself to heal at my own pace."

436. Temptations

Resist the urge!

Something self-destructive is calling out to you, and your angels rush in. They want you to see it for what it is: a test of your willpower. Journal about exactly what it is you are tempted to do. Reflect on what parts of you want it, and why. Try to see that the pain within is crying out for help, and that this isn't a good solution.

437. Dedication

Recommit yourself.

Your angels ask you to refocus and recommit to the dedications you stated early on in this journey. Revisit old goals, vision boards, or journal entries made when you first wanted to change your life. Allow yourself to see how far you've come.

438. Spread Out

Disperse what you have evenly.

One area of your life is feeling a bit lopsided. Your angels encourage you to see this and redistribute your time, energy, and resources to even it out. Where have you been neglecting one area of life in order to prop up another? Address this today!

439. Be Consistent

Avoid ups and downs with your lifestyle routines.

The inconsistency in your lifestyle routines is not going unnoticed by your angels. They encourage you to avoid overwhelming yourself, and choose the one thing today you can begin doing consistently. Don't add another new routine until you've mastered this one and worked it fluidly into your lifestyle.

440. Prayers

Connection becomes foundation!

Your angels applaud and further encourage you to feel the support of their divine interventions—and also see where it has shaped your daily life. Write a journal entry about how your life has shifted in some way since starting on your journey.

441. Absorb It

Breathe in spirit!

There is so much activity going on around you lately, it can be difficult to focus on the presence of your angels. Take short "spirit breaks" today. Practice deep breathing, take a reflective nature walk, or engage in mindful yoga stretches here and there.

442. Be Thankful

Be an angel to another person.

Take a moment today to thank your angels for their support, love, and guidance. Be an angel to another person today in the spirit of this gratitude. Treat someone to a coffee, send a thank-you note, or give a compliment to someone who could use it.

443. Worth It

You are your best investment.

The time you spend on yourself is not wasted. You are your best investment of time and energy. Your soul has a plan, and the best version of you needs to carry it out. Lie in meditation with your hands on your solar plexus chakra (just above the navel). Repeat this mantra: "I am worthy."

444. Protective Magic

Your prayers are heard.

This number assures you that you are being heard. Your angels are guiding you, surrounding you, and answering your prayers of protection. It may be a time of struggle, but you are being led into the light by your guardians. Take a moment to thank your angels for their protective presence in your life.

446. Lost

This was not in vain!

The material thing that you've lost is being acknowledged. Your angels are consoling you. And they are suggesting that you use this loss as a lesson so it was not in vain. Contemplate what this taught you today and allow yourself the space to feel whatever you need to feel.

445. Divine Timing

Let go of control.

When your angels intercede on your behalf, they will do it in divine ways, purposes, and timing. Your work today is to let go of control of how it all will come to you. Write down what you want on a piece of paper. Place the paper outside where nature can carry it away, symbolizing your ability to release control.

447. Stop Stalling

There's no time like the present.

The time is never better than now to move forward in a situation that keeps coming up. Your angels alert you that stalling and avoidance are not going to work this time. Make a plan to deal with it and take one step forward today, no matter how uncomfortable it may be.

448. Rest

Take a deep breath in and out.

What you need assistance with is being taken care of now by your angels. There are unseen forces at play that have taken over your cause. All they need from you is your faith in divine timing. Demonstrate peace today by meditating, taking a long bath, or just resting quietly in silence.

449. Be Aware

Angels are speaking to you!

You are being asked to open up your awareness to divine messages. They come in curiosity, in bursts of interest and moments of joy. Instead of shutting down your curiosity today, follow it. See where it leads you and take note.

450. Love Plan

Clear your schedule for love.

The priority today via your angels' urging is to spend focused time improving the quality of love in your life. Start by showing some self-love! Take some well-deserved "me time" today and know there is much more love coming your way.

451. Advice

Signs are everywhere!

Your angels are around you with strong messages about how to proceed in a tricky situation. They will use anything they can to reach you. They can be crafty, so prepare to be surprised. Repetition is your angels' favorite way to hit a message home.

452. Inspire

Inject inspiration.

Your growth needs some inspiration injected into it. Forget what you "should" do today and focus on what you want to do instead. Pick up an interesting book, create art, or update your vision board with new images and words that inspire you.

453. Divine Release

It's not working; try something new.

The things that you feel are out of hand presently are much too big for you to handle alone. Your angels encourage you to give them to your higher power to figure out. Let go of the things you are trying to do all at once, and focus instead on what *you* can control.

454. Isolation

You were never alone!

The challenges you've faced may have left you feeling isolated. Your angels want you to know that you were never without their love and support. Lie in meditation today and visualize a white light entering your body; know it is the love of the divine.

455. Pause

Enjoy this moment.

Your angels acknowledge that there is presently a pause in your life—a bit of a limbo. They assure you that this is a peaceful moment right before things change. Take a moment today to breathe. Throughout the day, work on breathing in and out, savoring where you are in the world right now.

456. Positive

The path is long, but you're on it!

You are experiencing some positive redirection in your life. And no matter what it looks like right now, rest assured that it's going the way you need it to. You are on a pathway to your best life. Several times throughout the day repeat this mantra: "I trust the divine to lead me."

457. New Light

Clarify romantic intentions.

A person in your romantic life needs to be seen in a different light. Your angels ask you to look closer at this person and really understand their motives and intentions toward you. Take time today to see, listen, and understand this relationship.

458. In Person

It's time for human-to-human connection!

Your angels want you to work on your interpersonal skills. Human-to-human connection is necessary in your life presently. Make a plan to meet with a friend, attend that happy hour you've been dodging, or get to your book club this week in person.

459. Kindness

Have a soft heart.

You are being asked to have a softer heart toward the world around you. The feelings of "me versus them" are not necessary. You have the control to create boundaries. Where can you demonstrate compassion and empathy to a person who is in need of it today?

460. Forgive

Let go and move on.

The resentments you are holding in life are only hurting yourself. Lie in meditation and picture the face of someone who has hurt you. Say what you need to say to them and then forgive. Know that their higher self will move on, and you will too, freer and lighter!

462. Reality

Consider others' perspectives.

You are being asked to look around and have a fundamental check-in with reality. Look at how you are being treated, who has been acting distant, and where you aren't being welcomed anymore. Make sure that how you view yourself is in line with how others view you.

461. Listen Carefully

Ask others about themselves.

Your angels are asking you to get personal about the ones you love. Ask them questions and really listen to their answers. Today, make it about them. Choose someone in your life who has been a little quiet and show them you care deeply about their lives.

463. Show Up

Your presence matters.

Your angels ask you to demonstrate support and stability for others simply by showing up. Worrying that you won't know what to say or do can hold you back from being the friend you want to be. Think of how you can support others today just by being there.

464. Parallels

Create a bond with the divine.

Include your angels in your intentions. They want to become a closer part of your journey. Building a relationship with the divine is what you are being called upon to do now. While lying in meditation today, repeat this mantra: "I welcome the connection to the divine."

465. Personal Wisdom

Be a role model for vulnerability.

You are being asked to model transformation. Be vulnerable with your emotions and thoughts with others who need to feel safe doing the same. Be proud of what you've accomplished in your spiritual awakening! Share your personal wisdom with someone who may need it today.

466. Present Gifts

There is only this moment, now.

Your angels remind you to stay here, in this present moment, in order to make the best of the blessings in your life. Show appreciation today for this present moment, and know that in doing so, you allow more blessings to find their way to you.

467. No Judgment

All emotions are welcome here!

Your angels want you to lovingly acknowledge and accept all your feelings. Treat them like guests in your mind, and listen to what they need to say to you. Sit with a difficult emotion today, and know that by doing so, you are learning more about yourself in a gentle way.

468. Renew Yourself

Every day, every moment, is a chance to start anew.

The pain and suffering of the past that come up in present moments are not going to control you anymore. Your angels support your journey to learn from this instead of simply being afflicted by it. Repeat this mantra: "I renew myself."

469. Reach Out

Don't suffer in silence.

Your angels are asking you to reach out. Your present circumstances call for support, guidance, and love. You are not alone: You are surrounded by people and places that can hold you right now. Reach out to someone close to you, or to a professional if need be.

470. Surrender

Release a problem!

You are being encouraged to surrender a present worry you have to your angels. Whether you are confused, feeling out of control, or simply at a loss for solutions, you can energetically release this issue to the divine. Repeat this mantra: "I surrender this to my angels." Trust that insight will come.

471. Solitude

Silence the noise.

There is a lot of activity and noise around you recently. Today your angels are asking you to cultivate solitude. Try meditating alone for ten minutes, taking a solo nature walk, or choosing a few hours this evening to disconnect from technology.

472. Feeling Alone

Explore your empath abilities.

Your angels acknowledge that lately you've been feeling alone, left out, and misunderstood. They are pushing you to explore these feelings more deeply by connecting to your empath abilities. Spend time today with a friend who gets it, read a book about this subject, or simply journal about how you feel.

473. Release Emotion

Allow yourself to emote.

As the stressors of life pile up around you, your angels are calling upon you to feel your feelings. The things you hold on to can hold you back and make you feel worse. Journal your feelings honestly today without judgment. Release them all to your angels and unburden yourself.

474. Distinguish Energies

Focus on your emotions!

There are many energies from many sources infiltrating your own. Your angels want you to focus on the feelings of others as they differ from your own feelings. Several times today, write down how you feel. Then contemplate where these emotions originate from.

475. Revisit Pain

Let go of guilt.

There is a need for you to revisit a circumstance of the past that is making itself known presently. Focusing on it with a different perspective will allow you to take what lessons are necessary and let go of the rest. Journal today about your feelings.

476. Clairvoyance

You are connected!

Heightened senses are coming to you as you shift more into your authentic self. You always had the connection to the divine, it's just more uncovered than ever. Lie in meditation with your hands on your third eye chakra (the center of the forehead). Repeat this mantra: "I see."

477. Visualize Harmony

You don't have to do this alone.

The fears you have are not supposed to be yours alone to hold. Visualize your angels taking them from you. Sit in meditation and picture a bright light washing over you, evaporating all your fears. You are left with only peace.

478. Protect Others

Use your voice to help another person.

Your angels want you to pay special attention to the people around you who don't have a voice. Lend yours to them in order to protect their interests. Speak for someone today whose voice isn't as strong as yours. Make sure you are heard loud and clear!

479. Embrace Silence

Clear the mind.

There is so much noise around you right now. The pulls, pushes, and voices from all over are bombarding you. They block you from your most important connection to self and spirit. Take a break today and embrace total silence. Sit in a space of quiet and invite in clarity.

480. Rest Assured

This is part of a bigger picture!

Trust that this present circumstance is integral in some way to the bigger picture. Challenges as well as blessings are all part of your journey. Write about how a challenge you currently face is teaching you about your own resilience and determination.

481. Celebrate Intuition

**You are connecting
to the divine.**

You are being called to appreciate your inner wisdom! When you have a moment of realization, a clear answer to a problem, or the right words to say in the moment, celebrate yourself. You are connecting with the divine and channeling its wisdom to others.

482. Inspire Yourself

Ignite your passion!

The slump you have been facing in life is being addressed today. Your angels want you to look around to become inspired. Follow a person on social media who interests you, go to an art museum, or flip through a book with ideas that ignite passion. Let your energy align with an inspired vibration.

483. Inner Acceptance

Receive self-love.

The quickest way to find acceptance in your life is to first gift it to yourself. Your angels notice that you need to work on your self-talk and self-care. Lie in meditation with your hands on your heart chakra. Repeat this mantra: "I receive self-love."

484. Time
Your pain is seen.

Your angels acknowledge your pain. Time doesn't necessarily heal wounds, but it gives you space to learn how to live with what has happened. Visualize yourself five years from now. Focus on your feelings, surroundings, and mental state at that time.

485. Regrets
Don't dwell on the past.

You have been dwelling too much on past regrets. You cannot change the past. What happened wasn't meant to torture you, but to create learning opportunities in which you could grow. Write down a regret and what you learned from it.

486. Soul Speaking
Do what is right for you!

Your angels acknowledge that you have been hearing some criticism lately about your own thoughts and opinions. They remind you that it's important to do what is right for you. Write about the criticism you've been receiving and contemplate its value, if any.

487. Imagine
Contemplate what will be.

Your angels ask you to practice visualization. Sit in meditation for five minutes and allow yourself to visualize your daily world as if what you want has already happened. Feel your feelings fully, see the colors of your life vividly, and allow yourself to wonder at this brand-new world.

488. Strengths

Focus on what you *can* do.

You are being cautioned not to focus on your weaknesses more than your strengths. Instead of seeing what you cannot do, flip the script and look at what you can do! Write out what your strengths are in all facets of life. Nothing is too small to mention.

489. Share Intelligence

Teaching is a calling.

The calling to impart your wisdom to others is being channeled by your angels. You are being asked to teach others how to heal. Research ways you can do this today. Find a context in which you can share what you've learned to those receptive to listening.

490. Mourn Loss

Let it go with love.

It is perfectly acceptable to grieve the loss of what has ended around you recently. The people, environments, and ways of thinking of the past served a valiant purpose. Write down something you are sad about letting go, and place the paper somewhere the wind can carry it away.

491. Assimilate

You are strong!

The challenges of this time aren't for succeeding or failing: they're for learning. Your angels are letting you know that you are here for a bigger picture, not just the result of a current pursuit. Focus on the challenge you presently face and what you are learning about yourself within it.

492. Time Helps

You are loved.

The losses you've experienced in life are heavy. Your angels remind you that while time does not heal, it does help. As you learn to live with the new normal, your guides hold you in their divine love and light. Lie in meditation and feel their love wash over you.

493. Stay Realistic

Focus on the now.

Your angels caution you against creating storylines and narratives that are not based in reality. Keep your mind focused on the present moment and away from the hypothetical. Look at a current situation through a new lens today.

494. Share News

Include others in your joy!

Drop the awkward feeling you have about sharing your accomplishments with people around you. Sharing in their enthusiasm for you is necessary in raising your vibration and creating a more celebratory atmosphere in which your goals can grow. Share some good news with someone today.

495. Embrace People

Let go of expectations.

Letting go of perceptions of who someone "should" be for you to have a relationship with them is the message today. Your angels are sending new people into your life for you to experience an adventure with. Embrace these new relationships with an open mind.

496. Another's Perspective

Get constructive feedback.

An outside perspective from a trusted and loved source is necessary for your personal growth and self-awareness. Ask a person you have a good relationship with to give you both praise and constructive criticism regarding your patterns as a person.

497. Ignite Passion

Motivate other people.

The motivation you feel to work on a goal is contagious! You are encouraged to align with others and get them moving forward with you. Combined energy toward this goal creates focus and faster results. Reach out to others and ignite their passion.

498. Hold Dear

Tell someone you are thankful for them.

Your angels are directing you to let others know how much you appreciate them. Send a thank-you card in the mail, write a thoughtful review for a business you frequent, or have a heartfelt conversation with someone you are grateful for.

499. Renewed Outlook

Welcome new choices.

You are being encouraged to make fresh choices reflecting fresh perspectives. Much has changed since you last made some significant decisions in your life, and your angels ask you to keep that in mind. Journal about a choice you need to make and how it will be influenced by your personal growth.

500. Ruminate

Is it worth the risk?

Your angels acknowledge that you are losing your patience with a situation that isn't changing. They are guarding you against rash decisions made on a whim. You don't have to make a choice today. Give yourself time to ponder what you should do next. Reflect and journal on the feelings of dissatisfaction you have. What do they mean at a surface level? And how do they play into patterns of your past?

501. Unchain Yourself

Release the negative.

There is space inside you being used to hold the bitterness of the past. Your angels implore you to keep the lessons but to let go of the resentment. You don't need to feel bad in order to protect yourself from it happening again. Visualize the anger you hold and picture yourself giving it back to the place or person you received it from. Feel the freedom of not having to hold that anger any longer.

502. Reevaluate

Take a step back and think!

The plan of action you undertook for a problem at hand needs to be reconsidered. Your angels are asking you to take a step back and reevaluate so as to make some different choices. Take some time today to reflect on the bigger picture, and what you could do differently.

503. New Developments

Prioritize balance.

In order to balance your life, you may have to get it a little out of whack first! Your angels want you to make some necessary changes to the status quo in order to implement new practices that will promote more balance in the long term. Take some time today to brainstorm what needs to change in order to do that.

504. Disjointed

Check in with your core values.

Your angels acknowledge that the present circumstances are creating a feeling of ill alignment in your own connection with the divine. They ask you to look at your core values and see which of them might be jeopardized. When you see that, you can begin the steps to realign your life.

505. Necessary Shifts

Change is hard but divine.

You are being asked to do difficult things, but you are supported. It is for your highest good. Write down your fears. Then bury or burn the paper to release those fears to the universe.

506. Enlightening Questions

Ask others what you don't know.

There are people around you who have already been through what you are facing now. It's important and healing to reach out to them for advice and wisdom. Think about whom you can talk to, and how mistakes can be avoided simply by listening to the wise and experienced people around you.

507. Visualize Life

You will face your fears.

The life that is waiting for you will come after you face many fears and perceived limitations. Your angels want you to get excited about this! Lie in meditation and visualize what your life will look like when you get what you want. Feel confidence and pride in how you've grown.

508. Best Self

Do what you love!

The opportunities to be your best self come in doing what you love to do. You are being guided to pick up passion projects and creative pursuits that interest you. Create a plan to jump into something you love.

509. A Choice

Compare values and decisions.

The time is now to make a decision. Your angels encourage you not to sit on it any longer. Write down your goals and values and compare them against what your options are for the choices you have to make next.

510. Organize Yourself

Get your life in order today.

The changes you have asked for are on their way. Organize your life so that when they come, you are ready to receive them. Create a checklist today of things that have to be done to create the smoothest transitions possible. Tackle what you can in a calm and peaceful manner.

511. Inner Power

Unlock your potential.

Your angels are telling you that it's time to have confidence in parts of yourself you feel are weak. When you see this number, think of something you are scared of and consider doing it. Asking for a raise? Making a friendship closer? Taking that new class? The time is *now* to go for it!

512. Play Fair

There are three sides to every story.

In a present situation in your life, it may be easy to choose a side quickly. However, your angels remind you that the truth lies somewhere outside of individual perspectives. Model an example of compassion and fairness as you lead others to rise above jumping to an unfair conclusion.

513. Give Attention

Use your words carefully!

Tempers and passions are flaring around you, but you are being called to take the higher road. Using wisdom with your words in all interactions around you is the challenge your angels ask you to pursue. Repeat this mantra: "My spirit is tranquil." Remember to count to ten before responding to any emotional communication around you.

514. No Toxicity

Detoxify your relationships.

Your guides want you to remove toxic patterns from your relationships. There is a need to review a current relationship and make a change for the better. If you cannot mend it and move forward, it's okay to let it go. Light a white candle and thank your angels for protecting you.

515. New You

Reinvent yourself in accordance with who you have always been.

All the lessons you've learned and all the challenges you've overcome have brought you closer to your authentic self. It's time to honor that growth; in all you say and do, reflect the "new" you! Repeat this mantra: "In my actions and words I honor my authentic self."

516. Finish It

You have the energy to do this.

The obstacle in front of you will not go away without your attention! It's time to get this done, and your angels are delivering energy to you in the form of motivation. Tackle the problem at hand without delay. Make a list of what you need to do, and check off each task as you do it.

517. Brave Chances

Believe that you are capable.

Push yourself out of your comfort zone. Your angels are letting you know that the time is now to take a chance to better your future. Speak up for yourself, try a new thing, or put your best foot forward in a brand-new situation!

518. Healthy Change

You need to alter your lifestyle.

There is something in your life presently that isn't helping your body and mind. Your angels want you to focus on the wellness of your whole self, not just your spirit. They call on you to take care of an issue you've let go on too long. What is the body or mind health action you have been needing to take? Make the time to confront this issue today.

519. Self-Assured

You made the right choice.

That tough decision you had to make? Your angels see it. They are signaling to you that you did the right thing. Now it's time to release the self-doubt so you can carry on. Take a salt bath today and visualize all the stress of this choice leaving your body.

520. Say Goodbye

**It is okay to mourn
what has changed.**

The ending that you knew was coming is upon you. It's time now to accept change and mourn the things you cannot take with you. Create a time for yourself to feel whatever it is you need to. Repeat this mantra: "I am protected."

521. Be Curious

Learn a new skill.

Your angels use your curiosity as a tool. Follow it to where you need to go next, and all will be revealed to you. But first, you just have to have fun! Think about a skill you're naturally curious about and pursue it in some way.

522. Embrace Life

Your view will change.

The things you want will replace some things you already have. Your angels want you to face the residual fears that can hold you back when you ask for your soul's desires. Write down something that you are fearful of losing, yet know has to go. Burn or bury the paper during the next full moon.

523. End Toxicity

Stop a cycle.

There is a present situation that reflects a much larger pattern. Your guides want you to see it. Where in your life today can you stop a cycle of toxicity? Reflect on what it is that needs to end, and write down a boundary you can put in place to do so.

524. Resentment

Judge with your heart.

Your angels encourage you to embrace a perspective of unconditional love when seeing the wrongs others have committed against you. You don't have to keep them in your life anymore, but you can also let go of the judgment you have held over them. Write their name down, then put the paper out where the wind can carry it away...along with any lasting resentment you may feel.

525. Money

Wealth flows to those who already believe they have it.

Financial abundance wants to flow to you, but you must prepare your mindset for it. Feeling grateful for what you want as if you already have it is the key. Repeat this mantra: "I am grateful for everything I have that moves me forward with my dreams!"

526. Surrounding Beauty

You see things others cannot!

There is a world around you full of mystery and beauty. The way you perceive it is unique. Your angels validate your ability and ask you to show others what you see. Do something artistic today: Paint, write, draw, or sculpt something that speaks to what it is you see.

527. Attract Romance

You are a sensual being.

You are being called to intensify intimate connections in your life. Your angels encourage you to embrace this need, not shut it out. Lie with your hands on your sacral chakra (the lower stomach) and repeat this mantra: "I embrace the sensual energy within me."

528. Love Strengthens

Love is directed to you!

New love is entering your life, and if you are in a relationship, a bond will be strengthened. There is an opportunity for you to attract the love you want by demonstrating it to yourself. Today, show yourself love in an act of self-care.

529. Rebirth

Change your look, change your attitude.

What can you do to make your outward appearance match your inward desires for change? Try out a new hairstyle, wear a different color, or find another way to implement a simple change-up in your look!

530. Be Watchful

Make yourself safe.

Ensuring your personal safety is a way to practice self-care. On reflection, what behaviors or routines could be improved? Further examine the first one that comes to mind, and make a plan today to modify your own behavior in favor of personal safety.

531. Priorities

Reestablish what serves you.

There are relationships in your life that may not serve you in the long run. Revisit the time and attention you invest in those who may be toxic. Set boundaries for future interactions with people who know how to take but don't necessarily know how to give.

532. Absorb
It's never too late!

Your angels want you to improve yourself professionally. There are skills you know you need to acquire, and now is the time to take steps to do so. Make a plan today to take one step toward learning a new skill.

533. Change Up
Do something differently.

There is a repetitive pattern in your life that creates instability. See it, acknowledge it, and make a plan to change it. Journal the pattern you want to shift, and ask your angels for guidance in next steps to do just that.

534. Control
You steer your own ship.

Recent events could challenge the work you've done thus far. You are called to remember you are in control of your responses and actions. You do not have to lower yourself to match low vibrations. Lie in meditation and repeat this mantra: "I am in control of how I react."

535. Risk Reward
Try new things, carefully.

You can live adventurously without throwing caution to the wind! Your angels encourage you to try new things, meet new people, and take risks...but only in the interest of your highest good. Journal about what new things you'd like to try and give reasons for why they contribute to living your best life.

536. Express It

Make your voice heard.

Your angels encourage you to speak your love vulnerably and often to those you hold dear. It helps both you and the person who hears it. Think of someone in your life you care for deeply and create a moment of genuine connection with them.

537. Revisited Choice

Make sure it's right for you!

A choice or decision you just made is under a microscope now. Your angels want you to revisit that choice and make sure it's right for you. It's never too late to change your mind. Journal about a recent choice you made and explore the motivations as to why you made it. Were these motivations reflective of your highest good?

538. Intentional Energy

Don't waste a gift.

The abundance that flows your way is not to be squandered or gifted to places that don't benefit from it. Your time, energy, and resources are precious. Reflect carefully today on how you are using and distributing them.

539. Good Tidings

Angelic assistance is available to you.

The things that come to you are all in your highest good. Your angels feel your anxiety about handling new circumstances. Journal about all the fears you have, and feel the divine supporting you as you release each one onto the page.

540. Refresh

Renew your connection!

You may need to try a new way to connect to the divine so as to make it more impactful for your soul. Pick up a new spiritual podcast or book, join a local or online spiritual community, or engage in some sort of spiritual self-help journey to refresh your path.

541. Double Back

Review your choices.

The decisions of yesterday are being brought up in present situations. Take a moment today and review the lessons and subsequent choices of the past and contemplate how they are affecting you today. Ask yourself if there are any changes or alterations you need to make.

542. Self-Check

Give it your all.

Your angels encourage you to do a thorough self-check. They ask you to reflect on where in life you are holding yourself back. Reflect on the parts of your life you'd like to change but that you tend to convince yourself don't need to change.

543. Low Vibrations

Stay away from what brings you down!

You are being reminded not to waste your energy on low-vibrational situations. Drama, gossip, and conflict are distractions from your soul's goals. In quiet contemplation today, revisit goals you have made, and recommit yourself to them.

544. Inner Peace

Calm yourself.

The angst and anger you can feel in the present moment need to be addressed. It's okay to feel your feelings, but your angels remind you to take inventory of them. Do an outdoor activity that channels your stress into physical motion.

545. Ready Yourself

**Revisit an aspect of
your life today.**

You are not quite ready to take the next step. Your angels ask you to revisit a foundational aspect of your life and invest time and energy there. This could be a health matter, a relationship, or an area of financial organization. Take time today to get this situation settled.

546. Counsel

Consider the source!

Today you are being alerted to opinions and counsel that may not be in your best interest. Always consider the source when taking advice from another person. Review your own emotional state, what the other person's interests are, and whether the advice is in line with your highest good.

547. Authentically You

Speak your truth!

The time has come to reveal to yourself and others something you didn't feel comfortable expressing before. This realization of self has been with you for a while now, and your angels are ready to create changes in your life to accommodate it. Write a letter to your future self, describing how you feel in this moment.

548. Intentions

You have total authority over your response.

Your angels warn you against feeling you can control how others react to you in this life. The focus needs to be more on what you *can* control. Revisit your intentions and make sure they don't count on anyone but yourself and spirit to be realized!

549. Direction

There's been a change of plans.

The way you thought you were going has shifted slightly. Your angels are with you as you take in this change of plans. This is a challenge to stay firmly centered. Repeat this mantra throughout the day: "I am consistently connected to source energy."

550. Drastic Transitions

Change up your love life!

Whether you are single or in a relationship, your angels are alerting you to some drastic energy shifts. Be flexible for what is to come and know it serves your highest good. Get ahead of it today by repeating this mantra: "I am flexible and adaptable in love."

551. Life Change

Release your anxiety.

There is a colossal change building around your life currently. Your angels assure you it's for your highest good. Release any anxiety you have today. Take a salt bath, diffuse essential oils, and spend time away from technology.

552. Be Sure

Reflect carefully.

Something you've been focusing a lot of energy on needs reflection. Your angels acknowledge that you've been spending focused energy and time on learning a new skill set, but they want you to ask yourself honestly if this is what you really want. Contemplate this today in meditation.

553. Distractions

Reduce procrastination.

The things that come along to take you off course are being called out today. List the things that tend to create distractions and subsequent procrastination in your life. What are some ways you can reduce them and/or their effects?

554. Support Lines

Do not do this alone!

Your angels want you to ask for help! Not just from them, but from those around you. Asking for help opens yourself up to the hands of your angels. And with their support, what lies ahead will not be faced alone.

555. Major Change

Get your mindset right!

Change can be seen as a negative thing, but with the right mindset and the right alignment to your goals, it's actually your angels' way of readjusting your life to fit your desires. Life will look different when you get what you want!

556. Financial Redirection

It's *your* financial future.

You are being called to pay special attention to your financial situation. Your angels urge you to take a careful look at the reality of the situation. Today, get familiar with your financials, recent expenditures, and upcoming plans. Get in control of your financial future.

557. Expansive Thoughts

Consider a new perspective.

A simple change in perspective will shed light on the situation before you. Open your mind to hearing and seeing new interpretations of what you are currently dealing with. Your angels will work through curiosity, inspiration, and even other people today. Remember, when it comes to your angels, there will be a lot of repetition involved!

558. Welcomed Gifts

Take a look around.

It's time to celebrate your abundance! You have been working hard on receiving, and your angels are alerting you to take a look around and see where it's happening. List the recent gifts in your life that have been appearing in all forms, both tangible and intangible.

559. Important Change

You are the director of your future.

There are important changes occurring in your life presently. Your angels ask you to embrace them with flexibility and grace. Lie in meditation with your hands on your sacral chakra (the lower stomach). Repeat this mantra: "I am in control of my reactions."

560. Morals

Keep your core beliefs close to you!

While the world around you changes, you are reminded to hold steadfast to your core values. Your angels are warning you against giving up your beliefs and character for immediate gratification and convenience. Write about a value that you hold dear to your heart.

561. Get Creative

Show love differently.

The way you show love to someone in your life needs a little bit of pizzazz! Your angels are asking you to get creative in demonstrating your true feelings. Get romantic: Make a thoughtful outing happen or write something heartfelt and deliver it to them.

562. Emotional Changes

Acknowledge where you are.

Your angels are asking you to check in with your emotional state during this time of change in your life. They gently remind you that no emotion is wrong, but acknowledging it is necessary. Take some time today to reflect often about how you really feel.

563. Be Sensible

Build trust in yourself!

The most important person you have to build trust in is yourself. There are things in your life presently that ask you to demonstrate consistency and sensibility to yourself. Today, think of what you need to recommit to, with a promise of completion to yourself!

564. Release Drama

Serve your highest good.

You are being asked to let go of something in your life that no longer serves your highest good. This situation or relationship is bringing you pain and a cycle of repetitive disruption. Your angels want you to lovingly reflect on who you are when you are with or without this situation or relationship in your life.

565. Movement

Embody affection for others.

Your angels are asking you to join a movement that reflects the wisdom you've gained from your spiritual journey. There are like-minded people who want to encourage important change. Spreading the ideals of the divine as a group is what you are encouraged to do today.

566. Scaffold Life

It's *your* experience.

Taking control over how you frame a present experience is necessary. Your angels want you to ask yourself what you can get out of this and how it can help you in the long run. List your present challenges and what you want to overcome as well as learn.

567. Sanctity

Celebrate habits of enlightenment.

Habits you are creating in your daily life are bringing you toward a state of inner peace. Your angels want you to acknowledge that these practices have created a deeper connection with the divine. Write about one thing you've incorporated into your routine that has opened you up to enlightenment.

568. Schedule

You are being alerted by your angels to slow down.

This is a call for you to address your overwhelming schedule and let go of commitments that are not necessary. Take a close look today at your upcoming appointments, meetings, and social obligations and let go of the ones that bring you anxiety and dread.

569. Be Optimistic

Shift the perspective.

The changes that are happening are not all negative. There are parts to them that provide new opportunities, relationships, and connections that otherwise would not have been possible. Reflect today with a different perspective and see where the good lies.

570. Spiritual Ritual

Make it your own!

Your angels encourage you to make a spiritual ritual your own. Whether it's celebrating the full moon in your own special way, practicing a meditation in a favorite spot, or repeating a personalized mantra aloud, make the ritual unique to you!

571. Outsourcing

Make your own choices.

You are being asked to make your own decisions about present scenarios. Outsourcing your decision-making is limiting your control. Think of a present situation in which you need to be the person who calls the shots.

572. Difference

Your soul is calling you.

You have an innate desire to do good, and your angels are supporting you to start small in that passion today. Offer some wisdom to someone who needs it, volunteer time to an organization that could use it, or use your voice to speak for those who cannot.

573. Create Opportunity

Lend your wisdom!

The challenges you've faced were not just for your own personal growth; they were also for the purpose of lending support and wisdom to those who are going through something similar. Take time today to give back in some way to someone who could use this hard-won advice.

574. Different Approach

Break it down.

Change your perspective on a present problem you are facing. You can break it down into smaller parts to avoid being overwhelmed. Take a step back today from the actual problem and see it as a whole, then break it down into manageable parts.

575. Endless Possibilities

Concentrate on what is working.

Instead of focusing on all the negative things you feel could happen, move your attention to the positive things! Absolutely nothing happens in life without some good coming out of it, and today your angels challenge you to find that good, no matter how small it may be.

576. Teachers

Reflect on lessons learned.

You are being confronted with "teachers" everywhere you go. These may be new friends, strangers who approach you, or difficult coworkers. Your ability to perceive all of these people as linked to lessons is being tested. Write about a lesson you've learned from a "teacher."

577. Face It

Don't hold back!

The fear you have needs to be addressed head-on. A life lived in avoidance of what you fear is not a fulfilled life at all. Your angels want you to know that you are strong enough to handle what happens next. Think of how you can safely face a fear today.

578. Evolve Friendships

Surround yourself with like-minded people.

The people you surround yourself with affect your mindset. Your angels want you to embrace like-minded people who have interests that reflect the ones you are working on. Surrounding yourself with higher vibrations creates the life you want!

579. Energy Shifts

You will feel energized when you make a good choice.

Making a choice, even a difficult one, will feel liberating and leave you energized. Making a choice that is not right for you can leave you feeling empty, exhausted, and numb. Your angels want you to examine each choice and the physical feelings that occur afterward. Analyze your physical stamina today and link it to recent choices made.

580. Limiting Beliefs

**Narrate a new version
of who you are.**

Your angels want you to look closely at the story you've been telling yourself. There are parts of it that are keeping you from evolving into what your soul wants to be! Write positive thoughts about yourself on sticky notes and leave them in places you look often.

581. Undoubting

Don't shut yourself down.

You are getting a strong message to stop shutting yourself down. When you have a hunch, a feeling, or a burst of intuition, do not brush it off! Your angels want you, especially today, to take these feelings seriously and know they have deep meaning.

582. Inspiring Friends

Ignite new ideas.

Making a friend is more than just creating support around yourself. It's about igniting new ideas within. Your angels ask you to change it up with your friend group, and give someone the open-minded version of you. Let them change your viewpoints as you see things from their perspective.

583. Be Confident

Solve your problems.

You are being encouraged to solve a present problem on your own. It doesn't matter so much that you are successful but that you are doing it yourself. Think of a problem you can make a decision about and begin to solve on your own today.

584. Rearrange

Focus on you!

The things you walked away from left space that needs to be filled. You worked hard to cut attachments and ties, so now you are being asked to focus on self-care. Start a new book, creative pursuit, or meditation series today.

585. Scare Yourself

Get out of your comfort zone.

Nothing shakes up your way of thinking like doing something that scares you! Your angels want you to get yourself out of that comfort zone and lean in to the things you tend to avoid. Publish a journal entry, engage in public speaking, or talk to that person you've been too afraid to.

586. Truth

Do the difficult thing!

There is a present situation that requires you to stand in your truth. There will be criticism directed at you for doing this, and it may trigger your innate need to please others. Your angels recognize all of this and ask you to do it anyway. Repeat this mantra: "I stand in my truth."

587. Affirmations

Words make a difference.

You have the power to turn your current perspective around with positive affirmations. Your angels encourage you to live in reality, but to also see the sides of things that are less appreciated. Start with the daily affirmation "I am love," and increase the list of what you specifically love about yourself as needed.

588. Be Victorious

Focus on accomplishments!

Setting yourself up for success is what you are being signaled to do today. Create a list of what your main priorities are and tackle them head-on. Focus on your accomplishments and feel the reward of a successful day.

589. Higher Purpose

You are receiving divine inspirations.

You are called to a higher purpose. Your angels validate that your recent inspirations are of the divine and, when followed, will change the course of your life. Start today by lying in meditation with your hands on your crown chakra (the top of the head). Repeat this mantra: "I receive."

590. Gather Strengths

Focus on your talents.

You are encouraged to gather your strengths. You will need to focus on what you can do in the next chapter rather than what you cannot do. Create a list of your talents, reach out to a support system, and research next steps you can begin to take today in order to grow in areas you are proficient in.

591. Natural Fear

You are leaving a comfort zone.

The future is unknown, and your angels are validating the fear that comes with that. As you grow spiritually, you will be asked to leave behind the comfort of what you already know. Lie in meditation today and visualize the love of the divine filling you with peace.

592. True Feelings

Be authentically you.

The emotions you are currently experiencing are yours and yours alone. You are being supported in being authentic to them. Those around you who direct you to be different need to be avoided at this time. Write about how you feel without judgment today.

593. Positive Perspective

Look with new eyes!

You are tasked by your angels to approach a present situation with love, acceptance, and excitement. What was perceived in the past as daunting can be seen in a new light now. Reframe something that must be done with a positive perspective.

594. Disappointment

Don't let it take center stage.

The disappointment you feel does not have to take center stage. It's important to validate it, but your angels advise you not to give it more energy than you give the happy things that occur. Write down something you are disappointed about, and then something you are happy about.

595. Best Friend

Be your own admirer.

You are being directed to be your own best friend! Show yourself some self-care today in all that you do. Treat yourself to a spa day, write about what you most love about yourself, and reflect on all the people you've helped lately.

596. Set Routines

Honor your energy levels.

Your routine is not necessarily a standard 9-to-5 one! Your angels encourage you to track carefully what times of day you are most and least productive. Set up a routine that honors this natural rhythm you already have.

597. New Strategies

Be courageous when trying something new.

The goal you are attempting to accomplish needs a new strategy. Your angels admire your courage and say you'll need it now more than ever, as you will be asked to change your approach. Think outside the box regarding how to move forward in a new way.

598. Give Encouragement

Lift up another!

There is someone around you who is embarking on a new phase of life and needs encouraging words from you. Send a thoughtful note their way, pick up the phone and call, or if possible have a heartfelt conversation face to face.

599. Be Steadfast

Change your mind.

The present situation is calling you to change your mind about something. Being steadfast and secure in your own intuitive wisdom is necessary now. Write down what is important to you at this time and reflect how you can stay true to that in the days to come.

600. Unconditional Love

Family is everything.

Not everyone who loves you is perfect, but the unconditional love they give you is. Your angels want you to focus on the unconditional loving bonds of family. If it is something you don't have, they want you to create it. Who have you taken for granted that you can connect with today? Reach out to a family member on the phone, send a card, or pay a visit.

601. New

Embrace the unknown.

Your angels know you are stuck in a comfort zone, so a new opportunity is on its way to bump you out of it. Yes, it will be scary and unfamiliar, but it will also be good for you. Create confidence in yourself by repeating this mantra: "I am ready, safe and capable!"

602. Inspired Thought

Open up your mind.

As you decide what to do next on your current journey, your angels encourage you to change up your mindset. Thinking differently opens up pathways to new perspectives! Take up a creative pursuit, draw, or craft to get your mind opened up to inspired thought.

603. Financial Balance

Check your habits.

Your angels want you to feel secure and balanced in your state of mind, and your finances contribute to that! Take time today to get real about what is coming in and going out of your bank account. Make any organizational changes you can to improve the flow.

604. Core Beliefs
Connect to the values you hold dear.

Your angels guide you to reflect on the core beliefs that are most important to you and discover a way to create emotion with them. Identify one core belief you have and write about how it came to be and how you wish to see it grow with you into the future.

605. Develop Boundaries
Create healthy limits.

Too many times others' needs, emotions, and authority infiltrate your personal boundaries. You are being supported in creating limits for these energies today. Write down where you find yourself going against your own self for the sake of others. Brainstorm how you can set some limits to rectify this.

606. Adjusted Lens
Talk to different people.

Your angels ask you to look through the lens of the divine instead of the one of your material world. Talk to people who look, speak, and act differently from what you consider the "norm." Reach out with an open mind and see what you learn today!

607. Mishaps
Don't let mistakes stop you.

The mistakes you make will sting, but your angels don't want you to stop yourself just because of that. They urge you to move past the inevitable feeling of discomfort you'll experience as you move forward toward your goals. Repeat this mantra: "I can conquer anything!"

608. Intangible Assets

Measure your abundance differently.

You are being redirected to measure the abundance in your life not by your material possessions, but by the intangible values, goals, and assets you've worked so hard to foster. Create a list of what you value most that can be seen not by the physical eyes but rather by the heart and soul.

609. Adapt

It may be difficult, but it's not undoable.

You are more adaptable than you realize. Your angels show you that your current circumstances may be challenging, but they are not impossible. Take small steps each day to adapt to this new normal.

610. Love Yourself

Love attracts love.

Your angels want you to send more pure, unconditional love to yourself by modeling what you want to receive. Self-love will attract positive relationships into your life! Meditate today on what unconditional love in your life feels like in its purest form.

611. Communicate

Speak your heart.

Your angels are reminding you to communicate your wants, needs, and thoughts to the people around you who love you. Think of something that could make a relationship in your life stronger. Relay it to the person you love in a way they can hear you.

612. Important Work

You are building something bigger than you know!

The work that you are doing is creating ripples far larger than the present situation calls for. Your angels applaud your efforts and encourage you to keep going with faith and trust. Visualize the light in your heart extending out into others' hearts.

613. Speak Clearly

Be clear in communication with others.

Before you speak, your angels remind you to organize your thoughts. Prepare an outline for an important upcoming conversation to avoid miscommunication. Include what your goals are and what you would like the outcome to be.

614. Family

Build foundations of family.

Your focus lately has centered on building and reinforcing your family bonds. Your angels support you as you create a foundational unit of support and love. Plan an activity with family members, then carry it out with enthusiasm and excitement!

615. Loyalty

First be loyal to your authentic self.

Your angels are cautioning you against betraying someone very dear to you: your own self. The actions and words you say need to reflect self-loyalty. Think about a present situation in which you feel you have to go against yourself in order to please another. Journal a letter to your guides asking for the strength to self-advocate.

616. Diversions

Rise above the interruptions.

The material world is sending you many interferences, and they are taking you away from your soul's important work. This number is a call to notice them so they do not disrupt you further. Repeat your full name out loud three times as you call yourself back into the present moment.

617. Look Closer

The details matter!

There are specific details in your life that have gone unnoticed for too long. It's time to gather your awareness and pay them the attention they deserve. Consider a situation you are dealing with presently and spend time on it in detail today. Observe things you otherwise would have missed.

618. Self-Love

Take care of *you*.

You often put others first but may also tend to dismiss your own needs. Your angels ask you to practice self-love today. Allow yourself space and time to do something that makes you feel nurtured and appreciated. Watch a movie, make a special meal, or treat yourself to a little special something you've been wanting.

619. New Scenery

Transition is natural.

This is an alert from your angels that something familiar to you is undergoing a big change. It can trigger you because you may doubt your ability to cope with it. Journal today about how you are feeling in a truthful way. Feel the release of any heaviness when you say these truths to your angels.

620. Filter

Watch your emotional responses.

Your angels caution you to take a moment before responding. It is better to take a break in communication to gather your thoughts than to respond immediately. Meditate on a person you have a conflict with. Speak to their higher self with love and patience about the problems you are having.

621. Influence

Set your own standards.

Others around you are doing things that are not in line with your own high standards. Your angels warn you not to lower your standards to meet theirs. Journal about a character standard that is important to you and explain why.

622. Deep Truths

Speak from your heart.

Your angels know you have feelings you push down. These feelings need to be directed at who they are meant for. In meditation today, picture the person you need to speak to sitting in front of you. Have an honest conversation with their higher self in a space of light and love. Feel liberated from any heaviness.

623. Conclusion

It's okay to mourn what you have lost.

You have made significant changes in your life, and it can be sad to let go of things that once served you but are no longer needed. Take time today to reflect on something you miss, and allow yourself to freely express any emotion you have.

624. Waste

Put yourself to good use!

There are talents and lessons you have been awarded but are not using. Your angels remind you that you are here to make use of these gifts. Reflect on where in your life you are feeling trapped or tied down, and determine what you can do to use your potential to the fullest.

625. Anxiety

Ground yourself.

Your angels acknowledge the scattered feelings you've been experiencing. As things around you change, the stability within is more important than ever. Lie with your hands over your root chakra (the base of the spine), and repeat this mantra: "I am safe."

626. Renewal

The new you was always there.

Your angels are applauding the ways in which you've adapted. Every challenge uncovers a bit more of your authentic self. Do something today that represents your renewal of self. Start something brand-new! Take a class, plant a seed, or begin a friendship.

627. Hard Work

Your efforts are investments.

Your diligence shows the universe you value your time and energy. You will receive reflections of your hard work in the value of upcoming opportunities and relationships. Spend time in nature today reflecting on all that you've accomplished thus far; feel the benefits of past efforts soak in like the sun upon your skin!

628. Respect Finances

Invest in yourself by creating a budget.

To show yourself you value your own time and energy, you have to be aware of what you are doing financially. Your angels ask you to sit with your finances and review recent expenditures. Create a plan for spending in the future.

629. Confusion

You don't always need to know all the answers.

It's very human to want to have answers to all the questions around you, but your angels warn you against making assumptions to fill in any gaps in knowledge. This is a divine exercise in letting things go. Lie in meditation today and practice deep breathing.

630. Change Patterns

Do it differently.

The way it's been taught to you is not necessarily the best way. Your angels want you to reevaluate some patterns in your life that are not working for you presently. Journal about how one of your patterns is not helping further yourself, and ask your angels for guidance in next steps.

631. Unclouded Thoughts

Clarify your mind.

Scattered thoughts are running your mind. Your angels want you to differentiate their messages from your own fears. Lie in meditation with your hands over your crown chakra (the top of the head). Repeat this mantra: "I am enlightened."

632. Soul Rest

Practice alone time.

Distracting yourself with people, places, and things is creating distance from self and spirit. Lie in meditation, listening to sounds of nature, and as your thoughts and feelings pop in, take note of them but try not to dwell.

633. Realize

See what matters!

The imbalance of your life has shifted into more focus on the material world than the spiritual world. Your angels alert you that your interests lately are of this world only and not of the next. Create a spiritual practice in your life starting today. Think of how you can incorporate balance of mind, body, and spirit into this new routine.

634. Vibrational Blessings

The reward may surprise you.

Your rewards come in the form of peace, compassion, and freedom from concern about others' opinions. List which blessings you've received in the form of intangible feelings and character qualities.

635. Stagnant

Life grows in the peaceful moments.

Your angels acknowledge that life has felt stagnant lately. But that doesn't mean nothing is happening behind the scenes! What can you do to move things along today? Take a class, start a new project, or make a fun plan. Get life moving again on your own terms.

636. Assets

You can't take material things with you.

Shift your focus from making money to deciding what you can do for others once you have it. When you have more, you help others more. What wonderful things can you do with abundance? Make a small donation to an organization you hold dear, perhaps even in the amount of this angel number.

637. Contemplation

Fear is not a motivation.

There has been a lot of focus lately on the material world. Your angels note that fear has been driving you forward. When you take that away, what do you see? Contemplate what areas you need to revisit, as they have been touched by fear instead of love and faith.

638. Integrity

Truth sets us all free.

It can be hard to hear the truth, and also difficult to tell it. But your angels are asking you to do both now. The circumstances around you require you to be strong in both your receptiveness and responsiveness to honesty. Repeat this mantra: "I welcome divine truth."

639. Desire

Reflect on love and lust.

Your angels are asking you to reflect on some recent behaviors in love relationships. It's important to feel desire—as well as desired! Lie in meditation today with your hands on your sacral chakra (the lower stomach). Repeat this mantra: "I am desire."

640. Thoughtful Revision

Change up what you ask for.

The desires you wish to be manifested need some reviewing and revising. Your angels ask you to reconsider what is most important to you, and revise these things to ensure they authentically reflect who you are. Create a new list of goals and speak them out loud during the next new moon.

641. Pressing Matters

Make it part of your personal system.

Your angels note that with the influx of new information or resources, you have to incorporate new methods into your daily life. Make the calls, set up structures, or just redraft your routine to include this new information.

642. Money Talk

Abundance flows where attention goes!

Your angels encourage you to stay involved in your own finances. Paying attention to your money shows the universe that you respect abundance and manage it with care and concern. This paves the way for more abundance. Spend some time today reviewing your accounts, budgets, and interest rates.

643. Consideration

Honor the gifts you've received.

Show that you respect what the universe has gifted you by taking care of it! What can you do in your life to honor gifts, goals accomplished, and hard work completed? Make a plan today to treat something you have with more respect.

644. Struggle
Self-created stress is unhealthy.

Your angels are asking you to get honest about how you contribute undue stress and conflict to your own life. They ask you to contemplate how "struggle" plays into your comfort zones. Several times throughout the day, repeat this mantra: "Life flows smoothly around me; I am peaceful."

645. Making Space
Reduce physical and spiritual clutter.

There are things around you that need to go! Your physical world clutter reflects in your mind space. What can you donate, recycle, or throw away in order to reduce this? Start mindfully clearing your physical space today and notice the space you create in your thoughts and reflections.

646. Hard Times
Make a promise and keep it.

In the trying times that surround you, your angels remind you to keep your focus on what is important. They want you to take time today to recommit yourself to your faith that the universe will provide your desires. Throughout the day, repeat this mantra: "I am safe and protected."

647. Move Money
Financial blocks hold you back.

Your angels want to remind you that leaving financial things to figure themselves out doesn't work. You must take action, and today is the day your angels are pushing you to do it. Spend twenty minutes getting a plan in action for financially freeing yourself.

648. Material Things

**You are manifesting
on all levels!**

You are in a vibration where the material things you've been asking for are finally coming through. Clear space today for the things you want to invite in. Clean a closet, donate an unused item, or reorganize the garage.

649. Well Done

Revel in your triumphs.

You are being congratulated for a job well done. Your angels have noted that you've handled things as authentically as you could, and they encourage you to rest and rebuild from the effort you've put forth. Celebrate yourself today. Treat yourself in some way in honor of your accomplishment.

650. Show Affection

Celebrate self-love!

Your angels want you to show love to yourself today. How well you do this will reflect in both current and forthcoming relationships in your life. Treat yourself to a pedicure, amp up your skin care game, or just take a well-deserved nap today.

651. Home

Tackle the concerns!

There is an area of your home environment that needs more attention. This could be a relationship, an organizational issue, or something that just feels off-balance every time you look at it. Take initiative at home today by addressing the concerns you've been coming up against recently.

652. Practical Skills

Become busy.

Your angels encourage you to get your hands dirty today. They want you to throw yourself into a practical skill set. Get that garden going, paint the wall you've been staring at, or learn how to fix something around the house yourself.

653. Benevolence

Filter your words.

It's been a little too easy for you to respond in anger recently. Not only to others, but to yourself as well. Your angels ask you to contemplate the meaning and benefits of kindness. Journal about how you've struggled with this in recent days.

654. Slipping

Beware of old habits!

You are being asked to take caution today. Present events are causing you to slip into old patterns of behavior and response that you were doing so well keeping out of your life. Several times today repeat this mantra: "I am strong and steadfast."

655. Self-Power

Be your own advocate.

Try not to outsource your own power. As things present themselves to you rapidly, be mindful of what you delegate and to whom. Pay special attention to where you may be doing this in your life right now, and pause to reflect how you can be helped without giving your control away.

656. Interesting People

Create a soul connection.

Your angels are sending new relationships into your daily life. They want you to explore them with an open mind! Think of a new person in your life, and make a plan to get to know them better.

657. Expanding Circle

Get social!

It is time to expand your circle of friends and acquaintances. Your angels are encouraging you to get out and be social. Create links with like-minded people and be open-minded to the insights they bring you. Make a plan today to get social.

658. Financial Control

You've done well with money.

The sacrifices you've made on a financial level are paying off. Your angels are proud of you for paying attention to things you otherwise would have procrastinated about. Today, list the places in your life where there is less stress and more flow since taking control.

659. Seek Truth

Reflect on personal growth.

Personal growth occurs when you are able to be honest with yourself. Your angels remind you that no one knows everything, and it's okay to change your mind about things you once thought were true. Journal about what in your life is challenging you to embrace self-honesty.

660. Responsible

Act with common sense.

The rapid way you've been firing off decisions is under a microscope today! Your angels want you to make the responsible choice, not the easiest or most popular one. Your best tool is within you: common sense. Think of a way you can use common sense to make a decision you need today.

661. Superficial

The rewards are intangible.

The values and beliefs you hold dear are the reward, not the superficial material things around you. Your angels encourage you to redirect attention and focus to the intangible fruits of the soul. Journal today about a core value or belief you hold dear.

662. Big Picture

Make choices that reflect the main goal.

Instead of focusing on the little things that can distract you and create negativity, focus on the big picture today. Your angels remind you that when you keep that image in mind, each choice you make will be in favor of what you ultimately want. Write down your main goal and put the paper somewhere you will see it constantly.

663. Promises

Do not compromise your reliability.

Don't overextend yourself with promises you do not have the time, energy, or resources to fulfill. It's hard to say no up front, but your angels are asking you to do just that. Think of places in your life presently where you need to say no.

664. Coordinate Intentions

Core values take precedent!

What matters most to you is being examined today. Your angels ask you to align your intentions with your core values and highest priorities. Review your goals and revise them to reflect that which is most important to you.

665. Transformative Power

Show others the way.

Being vulnerable in your journey to connect to self and spirit is what you are being called to do. It's part of your path to teach others how to do the same. Connect with someone today; open up enough to hear about how they, too, have the power to transform.

666. Personal Responsibility

It's time to reflect.

This number can have very negative connotations to some, but from your angels it's actually a powerful reminder to stop focusing on the material world so much. This is a strong message from your guardians to take personal responsibility in your own life and ask yourself in all areas, "What do I need to do differently?"

667. Jealousy

Rejoice in others.

Your angels are noting that feeling envious of what others have creates an energy of scarcity and inadequacy in your own life. You are being asked to rejoice in others' good fortune. Think of someone who recently received something. Feel their joy; feel the divine showering them with love; feel a part of it.

668. Technology Break

Reconnect with self!

Smartphones, television, and other forms of technology are causing you to detach from self and spirit. Your angels are letting you know that recently these things are creating more anxiety than joy and connection. Schedule a long break today, away from all these devices.

669. Problem-Solve

Take decisive action.

Your angels don't want you to sit around feeling helpless. They are pushing you to problem-solve amid the present circumstances. You are being encouraged to take decisive action today to show yourself and others that you will take control where you can.

670. Natural Peace

Find the perfect vibration of nature.

The disconnect or numbness you feel right now will pass. You are supported by the divine even when you are having a difficult time feeling anything at all. Create a peaceful connection in your life today. Sit in nature and allow the perfect vibration of the earth's energy to infuse into your own energy.

671. Tolerance

Try a different approach.

There are people around you whom you perceive as challenging. Your angels want you to view this as an opportunity to practice tolerance. Write about a person who presents a challenge for you, and focus on your similarities instead of your differences. Think of how to approach them differently!

672. Fitting In

You are learning about yourself.

For you, fitting in may not be as important as you once thought it was. Your angels are acknowledging that in the present situation, it's okay to stand out. Journal about how you feel out of place somewhere in life, and what it's teaching you about yourself.

673. Fifth-Dimensional Thinking

It's time to level up!

Your angels want you to level up your thinking to the fifth dimension. You are stuck in mundane struggles and material-world values. Reframe your thoughts to what this means in the big picture—how it relates back to your soul contract and what valuable lessons you are learning at this very moment.

674. Sustain Energy

Notice your wandering mind.

Your wandering mind is being noticed today by your angels. Recognize when you start to drift away from the task at hand and immediately get back to your focused work. Try a mindful exercise today to help train your brain to maintain focus! Yoga, meditation, or deep breathing can help.

675. Community Knowledge

Be open to support.

You are being asked to reach out to people in order to get a situation moving more smoothly than it currently is. Outreach can be awkward, but today your angels point out its necessity. Make the move to connect to someone who can help you.

676. The Void

Fill yourself with knowledge.

Material things may not be giving you the satisfaction they used to. And the void you used to fill with them may seem alarmingly empty. Your angels suggest that you first notice this, then dive in. How can you fill this void with the intangible gifts of the spirit? Meditate, help another, or learn something new today.

677. Be Rational

The fears you have are natural.

It's normal to be afraid of things—it's your ego trying to keep you safe. Create a healthy respect for your fears, while at the same time understanding that they aren't always correct! List your fears and contemplate which ones are rational and which are not.

678. Free Mind

Release limited thinking.

Your angels encourage you to open up your thinking! Embrace every thought and opportunity with an abundance mindset. If money/time/failure weren't a consideration, would you want to try it? Brainstorm some things today you'd like to try with a new mindset.

679. Shadow Self

Heal your deepest corners.

There are parts of you that are triggered presently, which reflects unhealed wounds. You are being asked to address deep hurts that have been left unattended for too long. You are supported by your angels. Pray for their guidance, ask for professional help if need be, and give yourself space to heal.

680. Unified Growth

Working together makes us stronger.

As you grow your material world around you, combine your efforts with like-minded individuals who support you no matter what. When you see this number, list those in your life who are there to help you and reach out to them with a gesture of thanks and love.

681. Dreams

There are messages!

The dreams you've been having are not for nothing: They have meanings that are applicable to your life right now. Put a journal by your bed so you can record your dreams as soon as you wake up. If you have trouble remembering your dreams, ask your angels to assist you in recalling them.

682. Bravery

You are supported to be you.

It takes courage to live life differently. Your angels fill you with their support to live life bravely as you authentically are. Make a list today of the places you have feared being yourself; think of a small way to confront one of those fears today.

683. Self-Confidence

Solve a problem on your own.

Your angels are asking you to consider whom you have become dependent upon. While it's okay to turn to others for assistance, your guides point out that you need to work on self-confidence. Today, handle a small issue on your own and see how good it feels!

684. Emotional Energy

Separate yourself from draining sources.

Others' emotional energies are enmeshed in your own. The feelings, desires, and needs of others have become too influential over your own wants and needs. Pay close attention to differentiating your emotions from the emotions of others today. Ask yourself how you feel—then examine whose feeling that is.

685. Self-Sabotage

Be your own best friend.

You are being asked to stop the self-sabotage. The negative choices you make hurt yourself the most— whether it's the money you spend that keeps you up at night or the greasy food you eat that just makes you feel sick. Think of ways to be a better friend to yourself!

686. Self-Esteem

Stand firm in your needs.

There are core needs that you have been placing above material ones. The people around you may not understand this, and may even attack you for it. Notice who they are and where they are coming from. Stand firm in your core values.

687. Angels Speak

Stay inspired and curious.

Your angels speak to you in those moments when you are highly vibrational and open to new ideas. Pick up an inspirational book today, try a new age soundscape, or simply walk outside and allow your thoughts to wander.

688. Financial Abundance

Be in the know.

There is an urgent need to focus on your financial situation. When you clear up, organize, and manage carefully what comes in and what goes out, you are setting yourself up for clearer pathways to financial abundance. Get in the know about your finances today.

689. Owned Power

Value change over fear.

The healing work you've been doing presently is not unnoticed by your angels. They applaud you for choosing knowledge over fear of change. Lie in meditation today with your hands on your solar plexus chakra (just above the navel). Repeat this mantra: "I am powerful."

690. Present Priorities

Take action today.

It's important to focus today on your present priorities. Your angels admire your intentions and dreams, and they want you to take action in order to acquire them. What can you do today to reflect what you want tomorrow?

691. New Things

Appreciate the learning curve.

There are many new things you are being asked to do. You are reminded by your angels that perfection isn't necessary. Lower your expectations as you experience a learning curve. Repeat this mantra: "I am excited to learn new things!"

692. Watch Habits

Beware of negative distractions.

The losses you've experienced cannot be numbed with toxic habits or self-destructive tendencies. Your angels warn you against overspending, drugs and drinking, and other forms of negative distractions. Sit in your feelings and write them down, take a walk, or start a creative pursuit instead.

693. Inner Self

Renew your spiritual goals!

You are being directed to refresh your goals! The dreams and intentions you have need to be firmly rooted in your authentic self. Your angels caution against putting too much emphasis on material goods and rewards. Write three goals that emphasize your inner self-growth.

694. Success Mindset

Use daily reminders.

Your mindset for success needs a solid framework. You are being directed to take what you want and make it a daily reminder. The more aware you are of your mindset, the better you can utilize it to live your best life. Write down your thoughts, intentions, and gratitude daily.

695. Show Initiative

Make the first move!

You can make the first move in life. Your angels are directing you to volunteer for that open position, call a person you want to get to know better, or simply be the first person to make an introduction. Show initiative to yourself and the universe.

696. Get Uncomfortable

Learn you're a survivor.

Your self-awareness of confidence, strength, and ingenuity needs to be made clear. Take a tough workout class, go somewhere you don't know the language, or put yourself in an activity you know is not your strong suit. See how you survive it, and take note of how you do just that!

697. Volunteer

Elevate your perspective.

There is a need for you to focus less on the superficiality of the world you live in and level up to a more spiritual level. Your angels ask you to involve yourself in a cause larger than your own. Volunteer your time to a worthy organization and share information with others on how to get involved.

698. Declutter

Revive your clarity.

Your angels encourage you to declutter your life! Tackle that closet, garage, or storage unit you've been letting sit for too long. Gift what you can to those who are in need. Feel the decluttering start to happen in your mind space as it happens in your physical space.

699. Adjust

Change your course.

The present situation is not going as planned and won't suddenly fix itself. Instead of focusing on the things that aren't working and that you cannot control, your angels encourage you to change your course of action. Brainstorm ways you can adjust yourself so as to make this experience better.

700. Originate

Your thoughts create your reality.

There is bravery in wanting something in life: You can get disappointed. Your angels want you to take that chance. What is it that you want? They are sending energy to you so as to manifest it in your life. Your work today is to want something! Write a closely held desire on a piece of paper and put it somewhere you can keep it safe.

701. Angelic Company

You are being protected.

Your angels see the struggle you are undergoing right now, and they want you to feel their loving presence supporting you. Call upon them to show themselves to you in signs and messages, and within the love and compassion of those around you. Ask them to show you their love, and believe it when you see it!

702. Eliminate Patterns

Make new choices.

Your angels encourage you to notice the habitual decisions you make on a daily basis and switch things up. Do something small today to rewire your habits of mind. Take a new route to work, order something new at the café, or start some small talk with a new friend.

703. Emotional Limits

You can say no.

Some people and situations in your life have become dependent on your prioritizing them over yourself. Your angels want you to notice your people-pleasing behaviors and address them. It's not selfish to say no. Journal about a present situation you feel forced into, and come up with some ideas about how you can create boundaries for yourself.

704. Evolved Beliefs

Establish new intentions.

Creating new intentions that reflect your evolved beliefs is what your angels encourage you to do today! Write down an intention that involves an intangible value you hold dear. Put the paper somewhere you can see it often, and speak it out loud under the stars during the next new moon.

705. Get Curious

Have fun with your journey!

Get curious about your moments of insight and revelation. Treating everything as an opportunity to explore is what you are encouraged to do. Have fun with it. Get a dream journal going, take note of the signs you see, and develop some full moon rituals.

706. Think

Reflect upon your growth.

You think differently than you did in the past. However, some of your behaviors and habits have yet to catch up. Today, reflect carefully on how you speak and act, and what your day consists of. Ask yourself if these things reflect the growth you've experienced. If not, think about what adjustments you can make.

707. Objective Observer

Conquer your fears.

You are called to be the objective observer of your own life. In order to get past any fears and limitations you may have, you first have to acknowledge them. Write down your fears and reflect on how to conquer them little by little each day.

708. Bounty

Shift your thinking.

You are being redirected to shift your mindset to one centered around abundance. The habits of mind that develop and strengthen with showing gratitude, seeing opportunities, and enjoying challenges will propel you forward. Repeat this mantra: "Abundance in all forms flows through me."

709. Do It

Fear cannot stop you.

You may be experiencing paralyzing fear and crushing self-doubt, but your angels say, "Do it anyway." There are opportunities right beyond the fear that require you to make the leap. Lie in meditation and visualize yourself having faced the fear. Feel how proud and confident you are in this moment!

710. Examine Carefully

Mistakes are our best teachers.

It's okay to look back on the past even when it's not comfortable. Your angels ask you to think back to a lesson that is coming up again today in a different form. In order to get past a current obstacle, you must learn the lesson it was meant to be! Journal about a problem you are having presently and how it connects to one from your past.

711. Persistence

Reap your rewards.

You've been working very hard at your goals, but at some point you have to take all you've done and benefit from it. Through this number, your angels ask you to honor your growth. Reflect on something you've been focusing on for a long time, and ask yourself how you can use it to create more for yourself today.

712. Self-Kindness

How you speak to yourself matters.

Negative self-talk is not necessary to keep what you have worked so hard to get. Create a list of five or more positive things you've done. Take a moment to say, "Thank you" to yourself as you read each one out loud.

713. Candor

Truth is what you speak.

It's getting hard to avoid that direct conversation you know you need to have. Your angels encourage you to speak kindly yet honestly. Prepare an outline of what you want to say; make sure to include your truth in how you plan to deliver it!

714. Effort

You get what you give.

Your angels are giving you a heads-up that an upcoming job won't be easy, but will be worth it. Ask your angels for a few signs that this is a worthy endeavor for you to begin. Keep in mind that with angels' messages, repetition is key.

715. Insightful Ideas

Embrace creative problem solving!

You are getting amazing insight into how to introduce creative solutions into your life! Not only will you benefit from this insight; the people around you will too. Write down some new ideas and creative solutions you've had recently; reflect on how to put them to use today.

716. Soul Companions

Important connections are building.

The people you meet are special to your journey. Welcome them into your heart space. Your angels want you to make new bonds so you can lend mutual support to one another. Make a plan today with a new friend.

717. Fortune Smiles

Take your prize!

A gift from your angels is being sent your way, so prepare to accept it. Fortune comes by way of good friendship, kind words, and opportunities that serve your highest self. See them for what they are, and bask in gratitude. Say a prayer today to your angels, thanking them in advance for the blessings they send you.

718. Be Wise

Make good fiscal choices.

Your angels are alerting you to watch your recent financial habits. It's a little reminder that honoring your money honors *you!* Take twenty minutes today to review recent spending habits and consider how the purchases you've made have either helped or hindered you.

719. Treat Yourself

Do something a little luxurious for yourself today!

Your angels have noticed that you've held back with giving yourself gifts and treats. Now they want you to demonstrate your faith by spoiling yourself a little. You don't have to spend a lot of money to prove you can treat yourself well.

720. Assistance Arrives

Acknowledge the presence of spirit.

The prayers you've sent have been received. Now it's time for you to receive the responses. Nature is the perfect way for your angels to gift you signs. Take time in nature today and observe what you see without distraction.

721. Focus

Review your goals.

The goals you've set may have fallen by the wayside, and your angels are reminding you to refocus. Write down three goals you have and put the paper in a place you will see it every day!

722. Restoring Acts

Clear your energetic space.

Your angels need you to cleanse your energy today. They acknowledge it's become too muddled with things that are holding you back. Take a salt bath, swim in a body of fresh water, or ground yourself by lying outside in the sun. Visualize anything that needs to go leaving your auric field (the energy around you that is also part of you).

723. Ponder Spirit

Center yourself today!

There is a calling from within, and your angels are asking you to answer it. Take significant time today and go to a place where you can feel centered. Distance yourself from technology, go into nature, and feel the pull of the divine within you.

724. Travel

Experience brings growth.

There is an adventure awaiting you, and it's in your highest good. Within new contexts and environments, your angels will bestow wisdom upon you. Plan a trip or adventure, no matter how small, and know that it's never a waste of time to see and experience new things.

725. Legacy

Be with those who make your soul sing.

You have a family, and you have also created bonds in your life with people who feel like family. Your angels want you to allocate time to spend with them. Create a plan to reconnect with a person who has always been there for you, and who perhaps has never asked for anything in return.

726. Elation

Keep your vibration high.

Your attitude is under a microscope today in the universe! How you respond will determine the way things will play out on a larger scale in your reality. Lie in meditation with your hands over your sacral chakra (the lower stomach). Repeat this mantra: "I am joyful."

727. Live Truth

Say what is authentic to you.

Your guides note that you've been holding back, not only from saying the things that need to be said to others, but also from saying what needs to be said to yourself. Lie in meditation with your hands on your throat chakra. Repeat this mantra: "I express myself; my voice is strong."

728. Be Open

Get out of your own way.

Ideas, inspirations, and messages are coming to you in order to serve your highest good. The fears that hold you back from the times you were disappointed need to be addressed. Write a letter to your angels about what scares you. Know that they hear you.

729. Appreciate Life

Be joyful today.

Your life is joyous; you are loved beyond measure by unseen forces, and you are here to do great things. Celebrate this life by planting flowers that attract and help wildlife. As you see the flowers being used, feel the gratitude and appreciation you have for this journey you are on.

730. Arrange It

Perfection is not a reality.

Your angels see you waiting to begin until things are exactly as you think they should be. But that's holding you back. Make a plan to begin today what you've been putting off. However small the first step is, make it—and celebrate it!

731. Positive Relationships

Like attracts like.

The energy you surround yourself with attracts more of the same. The friendships in your life need to reflect that which you want to bring forth. Nurture a friendship today that is representative of all that you would like to multiply in your own life. Be the friend you wish to have in this person.

732. Shift Reality

Luck is a mindset.

When you are in a negative mindset, negative forces are attracted to reinforce it. However, when you feel lucky, forces that reinforce that come in as well. Stop yourself for thirty seconds several times throughout the day, and repeat this mantra: "I am a powerful manifester!"

733. Don't Dread

Do it anyway!

The fear of what will happen when you get what you want is valid. But your angels encourage you to keep dreaming anyway. Face a small fear today. Speak up for yourself, wear a bold color, or pick a person you know could be a wonderful connection and ask them to coffee.

734. Dependability

We grow all the time.

The present situation is calling you to be personally responsible for your own role within it. Standing up and vulnerably expressing your part in all of it will set you free. Reflect on a current interaction in which it's time for soul growth in the form of being accountable.

735. Inner Child

Find the joy.

As a child, you didn't have to be told to play or have fun: It was your main goal. That child never went away; that child lives in you still! Be playful today. Get out a deck of cards or that favorite board game, or start an old-fashioned water balloon war with a friend.

736. Orderly Living

Get it done.

Your angels want you to address any loose ends you have currently and tie them up. It's time to finish what you started. Spend twenty minutes today addressing any projects you've been putting off seeing through to the end.

737. Move It

Take the initiative today.

The thing in your life that's at a standstill needs you to take action! The relationship that isn't going anywhere, the job where you feel stuck, or the home you need to move out of is calling to you. Think about what it is you wish was different and take action toward a change today.

738. Inner Solace

Feel one with the universe.

Today, quiet the mind. Your angels have messages to share with you, but fears and preoccupations will cloud your ability to receive them. Spend time in nature today, walking or sitting. Level your vibration to meet that of spirit and ask your angels to speak to you.

739. Feelings Check

Rein in your thoughts.

The scattered emotions you've had lately are affecting your vibration. It's okay to feel your feelings, but acknowledging them more intentionally is something your angels want you to spend some quality time on. Three times today, write down three feelings you have. Reflect on what they mean and where they originate.

740. New Connections

Keep an open mind!

People are showing up in your life who reflect the goals you've been putting forth into the universe. Meet them and open yourself up to what they have to teach you about life and yourself. Demonstrate that you have an open heart and mind to new connections by making a plan with a new friend.

741. Be You

Your authentic self takes work.

Your angels are noting that you feel unacceptable the way that you authentically are. Acknowledge it and see where this feeling originates. Write a journal entry about how you can feel out of place at times; ask yourself who and what makes you feel more authentic.

742. Undaunted

Have faith in your choices.

Your feelings are valid, and the choices you make because of them are important. A recent decision you made because of your emotional health is being applauded by your angels. Lie in meditation with your hands on your throat chakra and repeat this mantra: "My voice is strong."

743. Inspired Ideas

Refresh your thinking.

Refresh your thinking by incorporating new ideas. Your angels encourage you to expose yourself with an open mind to new thoughts, ideas, and messages so as to evolve your own! Pick up a book, take a class, or join a new community of like-minded individuals focused on self-growth.

744. Bravely Embrace

Your angels do things their way.

The answer you've been looking for is coming, but it may take some getting used to. Prepare yourself to be adaptable to the forthcoming solutions. Light a candle and take deep breaths in and out, releasing fear with each exhale.

745. Positive Affirmations

Speak from faith, not fear!

Your angels guard you against making plans based upon fears. Look at your goals, dreams, and wishes. Are they fear-based? Restate all manifestations on your vision board and in your journal as positive affirmations, and eliminate all negative affirmations.

746. Big Decisions

The steps you must take have been revealed.

The choice you need to make presently has already been decided in your heart! Your angels validate that you know what to do; looking within is the only work that is left. Today, ask the answer to reveal itself in meditation.

747. Upgrade

Speak to your higher self.

In order to get where you are today, you had to amp up your personal power. Your angels are patting you on the back for a job well done. Sit in meditation and visualize your own higher power. Speak kindly to your higher self, allowing your subconscious to merge with your superconscious.

748. Fearless Energy

Create intentions for your authentic self.

Abandon your fears at the door: You are creating intentions that will shape your life! Create an intention today that reflects something you are afraid of wanting for fear of disappointment or others' reactions to it.

749. Character

Reflect on foundations of self.

What character traits do you need to work on? Your angels ask you to visit the foundations of a quality you want to be known for. Meditate today on a character trait such as generosity, honesty, or fairness—anything you wish to represent. In your journal, list some goals you can aim for to affirm one of these traits.

750. Limitless Love

Love yourself and others freely!

Your angels are asking you to practice unconditional love today—not only for others but for yourself as well. Journal about the vulnerability that occurs when demonstrating unconditional love to yourself and others.

751. Be Inspired

Insert wonder into your life.

Your angels want you to experience more curiosity and awe in your life! There are forces around you that want to be let in through creative outlets. Take time today to allow yourself to be inspired. Read a new book that interests you, contemplate a poem, or sketch an image you see in nature.

752. Try

Learn something new.

There is something you want to do deep down but feel you will never be able to do. Your angels remind you that you don't have to be an expert at something to do it. Just go for it because you want to! Learn something new that you never would've thought you could do.

753. Reroute

It's okay to make a change.

A daily routine or healthy habit has been discarded, and your angels are pointing to it, asking for you to pick it back up. What are some ways you can reincorporate this daily routine so as to make it consistent once again?

754. Embrace Failure

Be fearless in new endeavors.

Your angels want you to know that whether a current endeavor ends in success or not was never the point. The point was for you to learn about yourself. Write a journal entry about what it is you want to do but have trepidations about. Be honest about the real reasons for your hesitation.

755. Unfamiliar Territory

Make yourself at home!

The world around you that you created feels awkward and unpleasant at times. But that is just because it is new. Your angels acknowledge this feeling. Familiarize something today. Make a friend, make a new space your own, or put your unique spin on an existing idea that you've encountered.

756. Unshackled

Nurture your desire.

The universe wants to align your journey to your soul contract, so let it. It's easy to want things, but hard to let go of control over the process of how that happens. But this is what your angels are calling on you to do today. Write down something you desperately want and bury the paper with a seed. Know that as you nurture the seed and watch it grow, so, too, does your desire grow into fruition.

757. Claircognizance

Welcome spiritual downloads.

The realization you are presently having is a game changer! Your angels are acknowledging that you've downloaded some major spiritual insight that is going to create ripples of change in your own life. Several times throughout the day repeat this mantra: "I accept divine wisdom."

758. Mood

Do a mental health check.

You are being asked to check in with your emotions and overall mental state. This is an alert from your guides to take all of this seriously. You are not alone, and others want to help you. Feel around today to see if you could use some extra support. If you feel you do need it, ask.

759. Paralyzed

Fear holds you back.

Your angels remind you that your fear is not proof of either success or failure. It's simply a creation of your own mind. Take action today toward the thing you are scared of, and know that the fear you carry with you is an indication that you are pushing the boundaries of your comfort zone—and that this is how great things get done!

760. Patiently Hear

Listen rather than speak.

This is a situation where your opinion might be better off kept to yourself. Write a journal entry in which you don't hold back on anything you think or feel, and reflect on what help it would be, if any, to share these thoughts and emotions.

761. Promise

Prioritize yourself!

You are being asked to make a promise to yourself to prioritize your time more efficiently. The energy and resources you have are being depleted by your need to accommodate everyone. Make a list of what your priorities are as opposed to the things that can wait.

762. Self-Assess

Improve your ability to welcome change.

In order to welcome in what is new and good, you need to know that you will be able to handle it when it arrives. Today your angels want you to assess your strengths and weaknesses and consider what it is you can do to improve today.

763. Fulfill Roles

See this to the end.

Your angels are signaling that you feel overwhelmed and over-extended. They want you to use this as a lesson not to overextend yourself in the future. Get a plan to quickly finish what you started, and reflect on how not to get into predicaments like this moving forward.

764. Release Fear

Uncover the truth hidden behind trepidation.

The fears that are ingrained in you need to be uncovered. They are quietly holding you back from living your most authentic life. They disguise themselves as truths, so the work to release them is challenging. Write down a fear you have, and burn or bury the paper during the next full moon.

765. Open-Hearted
Teaching others propels you forward.

When you teach others what you've learned, you, in turn, clarify your own takeaways. It reinforces your own journey as you take the time to explain it. Today you are being called to lightwork (spiritual work in service to others), by thinking of a way to teach others the wisdom you've gained!

766. Your Vision
Be honest about your motives.

Pay close attention to your own intentions, which are fueling all your actions and words. In contemplation today, double-check that you are being honest about your intentions and also that they are in line with what you want to happen overall.

767. Embrace Insight
Elevate your life.

You are being asked to elevate your life through self-education. Your angels want you to reach new levels of enlightenment through exposure to new ideas and perspectives. Pick up a book that interests you, listen to a new podcast, or have a thoughtful conversation with a friend today.

768. Spiritual Clutter
Release repetitive thoughts.

Unpack your mind's clutter by writing down, without judgment, all the thoughts that pop up today. Take a look at them reflectively and see where they originate. Acknowledge each one and release the negative ones with love, for they came to deliver a message, and you received it.

769. Your Authority

Remain flexible!

Ask yourself today where you do and do not have control. The changes flowing around you are going to settle eventually into a cycle of routine, and your angels remind you to remain adaptable and flexible until then. Repeat this mantra: "I am adaptable."

770. Improve Intuition

Practice your clairvoyance.

You have the ability to connect with the divine on many levels. Practice using your intuition today in places where it is fun and easy. Think of what color a coworker will wear to work, what your friend will order at lunch, or even what model car you'll see next on the road!

771. Transparency

Beliefs are important.

Your angels are asking you a question: "What do you believe?" Your path will become clear when you organize how you view the world and what your role here is. Write a list of things that you feel are very true, and a list of things you are not so sure about right now.

772. Think Thoroughly

Take time to respond.

The importance of thinking things through is being emphasized by your angels today. A present situation calls for you to give ample energy and time in order to form an appropriate response. Contemplate all aspects of what is going on around you, and remember that it's okay to take time to process things before responding.

773. Continued Work

Take a break today, then keep going.

Your angels are encouraging you to push through this challenge to completion. It's okay to take a break; just don't give up! Make a list of what you need to do in order to finish what you started. Then take a break today while you replenish your energy to begin again tomorrow.

774. Relevance

Inspect further.

You need to see something in a new light. A present circumstance is being handled in a way that actually may be creating more work for you. Take a closer look today at what is going on around you, and ask yourself if what you are doing is relevant to solving the problem.

775. Soul Contemplation

It's not about being the best.

It's not about winning, or even being the most successful. It's about the experience and what it teaches you. Your angels want you to reflect on a present situation and rethink what "success" is within it.

776. Body Check

Your physical self mirrors your spiritual self.

Your body is responding to the spiritual awakening you are undergoing. Your angels want you to notice this and document what you feel and experience. This could include vivid dreams, an intense connection to nature, or a heightened sensitivity to smells and sounds.

777. Face Fear
Trust the divine.

Your angels are asking you to release the fear of the unknown, to trust the universe and give up your control of what's going to happen next. Your angels are telling you to not fear the future but rather to embrace it with faith that it's all in your best interest. It is perfect in the design brought to you by your most trusted guardian angels.

778. Relish Life
You already have so much!

You are being asked to look at all you have in life and really relish it today. By doing this you increase your ability to receive more. Feeling gratitude instead of lack creates the vibration of abundance. List five things you are grateful for right now.

779. Higher Self
Evolve yourself.

The relationship with your higher self is of the utmost importance. Your angels are encouraging you to do the work to evolve yourself. Clear mental clutter through meditation, choose gratitude as a mindset, and give yourself space to heal old wounds.

780. Higher Vibrations
The things you think, you create.

Everything is energy, and the frequency you are at will attract the same from all around you. Raising your own frequency ensures that higher-vibrational beings and opportunities are attracted to you. Look to your mindset, self-care routines, and how you talk about yourself to others to raise that vibe!

781. Knowledge

New insight will change your life.

It's a normal response of your ego to shut down a divine realization or message because it can completely change your life. Acknowledge that the spiritual downloads you are getting may in fact change everything, and listen to them anyway. Repeat this mantra: "I welcome spiritual insight."

782. Old Beliefs

Open yourself to the divine.

There are many subconscious pathways within you that are holding you hostage from living life in the way your soul cries out to live. Release the old beliefs that have held you back and create room for new ones. Repeat this mantra: "I am open to divine wisdom."

783. Consider Values

You have evolved.

You are being asked to consider your own beliefs. The way you have evolved may not line up with the job you are in or the people you surround yourself with. Contemplate this today, and write down three values you hold dear.

784. Examination

Heal the wounds.

The toxic relationships in your life were latching on to something within you. You are being asked to realize what that "something" was and heal it. Ask yourself today what worked in a toxic relationship, and what did not. Examine what wounds were activated at that time.

785. Trepidation

Stop avoiding it.

Your angels note that you've been spending a lot of time and energy avoiding your fears instead of facing them head-on. They want you to first focus on what you fear most and then dive into it more deeply. Take a close look at it today and examine how it came to be.

786. Emotional Space

Assert yourself.

Boundaries are currently necessary in your life. You are being encouraged to be assertive when expressing them. You can be kind and still be assertive. Think of where a boundary needs to be set in your life and execute a plan to do this.

787. Automatic Writing

You are filled with wisdom.

You are being encouraged to do some journaling today and practice automatic writing. Sit in a quiet space and freewrite whatever comes to mind. Try not to judge it: Just allow yourself to write and see what unfolds on the paper.

788. Inner Narrator

Observe your self-talk.

Observe your thoughts and feelings carefully today. Play the role of "observer" in your self-talk. You are not your thoughts, but your thoughts do create your reality. Monitor them carefully and deep-dive into ones that seem to reflect scarcity and negativity.

789. Courage
You are brave!

You are courageous, and your angels are applauding you. The present circumstances that called upon you to be true to yourself were opportunities for you to grow. Journal about what you learned from a recent circumstance in which you had to be true to yourself.

790. Symbolic Closure
Drop the struggle.

You are being directed to create closure in a symbolic way. There is a situation you know is over, and you need a strong representation of its ending in your life. Write down what it is that you need to let go, then burn the paper under the next full moon.

791. Release Desperation
There is no timeline.

Timing is something that your angels are alerting you to let go of. They sense your desperation with an attachment to a deadline for a present goal or dream. Repeat this mantra: "I welcome what is meant to be mine in divine timing."

792. Deeper Meanings
Explore your feelings.

Your feelings are not anything to fear. They are with you so you can explore them and understand their deeper meanings. Take time today to write about feelings you have, and what their underlying causes may be.

793. Look Back

Revisit your mindset.

There was a point in time you wanted change, and you are being asked to revisit that mindset. Your angels want you to reflect and remember why you are doing what you are. Take time today to write down the pivotal moment in your life that reprioritized your goals.

794. Self-Invest

Prioritize your development.

You are encouraged to invest in yourself. The dreams and goals you have need to be realized by prioritizing your own development. Take the time, energy, and resources you can spare to take a class, training, or educational program that assists in this personal growth.

795. Immerse Yourself

Create connections.

Immersing yourself in another's world is a way to create connections to self and spirit that you couldn't have imagined. Volunteer with a group that needs you, take on the cause of something that speaks to you, or simply be a friend to someone you would not have otherwise crossed paths with.

796. Character Counts

Strengthen a quality you admire.

Think of a character quality you would love to improve. Journal about what this is and how you've seen it demonstrated in people you admire. Consider how you can create ways to foster this quality in your daily life.

797. Shifting Outlook

New priorities have formed!

The perspectives you've gained on your spiritual journey have undoubtedly evolved your priorities in life. Today, reflect on how far you've come. Write about what you have learned and how your priorities have shifted following these lessons.

798. Forgive Yourself

Drain the negativity.

Your angels encourage you to be more forgiving to yourself. The mistakes of the past are being dwelled on in an unproductive way. Gift yourself the time and patience you give others. Lie in meditation today and visualize all the negative energy you feel draining out of you into the ground below.

799. Repression

Examine your perception.

In this time of change you are being asked to rid yourself of limiting beliefs. The thoughts and feelings you have about yourself need to be carefully examined. Your angels want you to make a journal entry in which you sort through what perceptions are working for you and what perceptions are working against you.

800. Spiritual Downloads

Prepare for new knowledge!

Your angels are indicating that you will be receiving new information in the form of realizations, wisdom, and emotions. Create time for a meditation where you focus energy on opening your crown chakra (the top of the head) in preparation for this divine light.

801. Soul Renovation

Shed the past; awaken to your truth.

You have been through many trials and tribulations. Now is the time to put down the armor you needed to survive them and live freely. The door has opened to your new life. In meditation today, envision yourself walking through a doorway. What do you see? What does it look like when you are living your truth?

802. Your Choice

Use your own intuition.

There has been a lot of wonderful advice given to you, but now it's time to sit with your own intuition and make a choice that works for you. Take some time today to ponder. Write down how you feel in this moment, and use that as a baseline for what to do next.

803. Balanced Love

Spend time with a loved one.

A relationship that is important to you needs some nurturing. Balancing your life with the needs of this person is important. Create some time to spend with someone who means a lot to you; make sure to tell them what you feel from the heart!

804. Bona Fide Life

You are ready to live your values.

Living your values is a calling, one that your angels are signaling you are ready for. There is movement around you in the universe, with people and opportunities aligning so as to create a context for you to do so. Repeat this mantra: "I am ready to live authentically."

805. Eliminate Distractions

Receive revelations.

It's time to be distraction-free. Your angels want to deliver insight to you, but technology and similar interruptions bar the way. You are being encouraged to take time away from them today and see what revelations come to you.

806. Love Lens

You see others truly.

You are being applauded by your angels. The unconditional love of the divine is the lens through which you have been seeing the world around you. They ask you to speak of this view to others—to teach them how to use love as a way of life in all things.

807. Sincerely, You

Switch your mindset.

Instead of being fearful of the scenario you are presently in, try switching your mindset to be grateful for the opportunity you have to conquer this fear. Write a letter to yourself about how you feel now, and plan to read it after you've faced your challenges.

808. Rejoice

The foundation for your future is here!

The angels celebrate you. You are self-aware and focused on personal growth. The road has not always been easy, but you took control of your response to it. The habits you've formed are foundational for your future. Do something special for yourself today in celebration of all you've accomplished.

809. Reinforcements

Don't do this alone.

You don't have to experience a present hardship by yourself. There are people around you whom you can lean on. Their wisdom is abundant and available to you. Reach out to a trusted person to ask for advice and counsel.

810. Fiscal Responsibility

Value yourself.

Spending money on frivolous things that bring you neither satisfaction nor long-term joy is something to take inventory of here. Your angels call upon you to be more fiscally responsible so as to attract abundance your way. Take time today to map out a few changes to your spending habits.

811. Faith-Filled

The inspiration is divine.

All of those ideas and spiritual downloads you've been having are from a higher power. This number calls on you to take actual steps toward your inspired thoughts. Journal about a dream you have. Then list three steps you can take today to make it a tangible reality.

812. Attempts

Be open to all possibilities.

Your angels are sending you inspiration through various sources, but how you receive it matters. Keeping an open mind to new opportunities, relationships, and adventures is what they are asking you to do. What is something new you've been asked to do but said no to?

813. New Relationships

Make authentic connections.

A new relationship is entering your life, and it reflects your new-found authenticity. Your angels encourage you to begin it by being yourself. Repeat this mantra: "I am my authentic self."

814. Investments

The time was never a waste.

The investment of time and money you've put in was not for nothing, and your angels want you to focus on what it was actually about. Journal what your main takeaways were, and how they provide valuable insight that aids your personal growth.

815. Separate Yourself

Cut the cords that do not help you.

People who take your energy drain you of the ability to manifest what you actually want. Take a ritual salt bath today. Submerge yourself in the water and visualize all the cords others have placed on you falling off into the water, sinking to the bottom, and leaving through the drain.

816. Romance

Passionate love surrounds you.

An old love or a new one is heating up! Your angels encourage you to strengthen this bond and create intimate connections between you. Lie in meditation today and visualize a divine white light cleansing your heart chakra.

817. Passion

Follow your interests.

The thing you do that comes so naturally to you is your gift! Your passions are given to you so as to make your life meaningful for yourself and for others. You are being called to master a talent you already own. Think of a way to take something you are naturally enthusiastic about to the next level.

818. Infinity

Life is a never-ending loop.

One cycle in your life is ending, but another is beginning. It can feel catastrophic, but it's the natural way of things. Be on the lookout for other numbers coming your way: Your communication is strong right now with your angels.

819. Paying Forward

To give is to receive.

You are being called to pay it forward in some way today. Thinking of all the gratitude you've had for the blessings bestowed upon you will inspire you. Make a small donation of time or money to a place or person you know could use it!

820. Receiver

What you asked for will be delivered.

The gratitude in your heart creates the abundance in your reality. You are being applauded for your careful observation of your thoughts and words. Repeat this mantra: "I am the creator of my universe."

821. Opportunities

Your time is coming.

What you've been asking for isn't far off: It's just waiting for divine timing to come to you. In your meditation today, picture yourself floating in a sea of endless abundance; watch the waves of fortune flow through you and around you effortlessly.

822. Accept Prosperity

You deserve it!

The abundance coming your way cannot arrive unless you feel worthy of it. Clear pathways today in your energy so as to accept these gifts. Sweep any negative energy off your body using your hands, just as if you were dusting off a coat. Wash your hands thoroughly when you are done.

823. Demonstrate Love

You are needed.

There is a person in your life who needs your unconditional love. Your angels urge you to give it to them. Reach out in some way and be prepared to listen, support, and hold space for them today.

824. Enthusiasm

You raise the vibe.

The happiness you exude to others lifts the vibration of everyone around you. Your angels applaud your enthusiasm and let you know it's a divine gift you embody. Plan a way to include others in your happiness, be it a little luncheon or a simple moment of shared happiness.

825. Energize Yourself

Confidence is a wonderful energy.

As life shifts around you in your favor, your angels remind you to work on receiving it gratefully and confidently. Lie with your hands over your solar plexus chakra (just above the navel) and repeat this mantra: "I am confident and capable."

826. Blessed Soul

Speak your blessings aloud.

When you express your gratitude, it opens the door for more blessings to follow. Speak freely to yourself and others of how appreciative you are of the life you've been given. Create a list of what you are blessed with; repeat these things to yourself as you go about your day.

827. Joy

Your angels ask you to celebrate.

Be joyous! Your angels want you to have a lighthearted time today doing something that brings pure joy to your soul. Plan time today to celebrate your unique self with an activity that brings a smile to your face and heart.

828. Victory

Be content with what you've done.

Remember the sacrifices you made, the work you did, and the truths you uncovered. Your angels applaud you and send you celebratory energy. Show them you receive it by thanking yourself today. Dance and sing your happiest song. Feel the divine flow through you.

829. Enough

You will always have what you need.

Your angels notice that enough never seems to be enough. They want you to contemplate an area of your life in which this is apparent presently. Lie in meditation with your hands on your root chakra (the base of the spine). Repeat this mantra: "I am enough."

830. Start Small

How you begin matters!

The dreams you are creating live today as seeds in the microcosm of your daily activities. Do every little thing as you would if it were larger. Lie in meditation and visualize what life will look like when it reaps the rewards of your actions today.

831. Visualize

See balance in your future.

When you ask for abundance in one area of your life, picture how it will look in the other areas too. Create a vision board that represents the wants and needs of your body, mind, and spirit!

832. Remember

Your blessings assist others.

Your angels ask you to reflect on where you started so as to increase your compassion for those who are there currently. Think of a person in your life who reminds you of where you once were, and extend assistance to them in some way.

833. Long Game

This is a journey.

The new, balanced habits you've formed are not temporary: They are meant to be implemented for the rest of your journey on this earth plane. Let go of any timeline you may have that is attached to better habits you've gained recently.

834. Energetic Responsibility

Be aware of the vibes you send out.

Your angels alert you to be self-aware of the vibrations you are sending out. What you are going through is creating havoc for those who are absorbing your energy. Lie in meditation with your hands on your sacral chakra (the lower stomach) and repeat this mantra: "I am in control."

835. Recalibrate

Keep the flow going.

As one area of your life seems to be growing, check in on a stagnant area that is yet to evolve. What can you do today to recalibrate your life so as to create balance throughout?

836. Ripple Effect

The work you do today will benefit you in the future.

Every sacrifice, emotional response, and challenge you see through benefits your future self. Write a letter to yourself about the struggles of today and how you relate them to the hopes of tomorrow. Seal it and read it at a later date of your choosing.

837. Make Moves

Love is an action!

Your angels encourage you to make a move in love. If you are in a relationship, put more of yourself into it today. If you are single, make strides to connect with others. List what you can do to make more action out of love in your life.

838. Take Rest

Celebrate your achievements.

Celebrating yourself is the message from your angels today. They want you to sit in gratitude and awe of yourself and of the role the divine has played in your life. Think of something fun to do. Make a date with a friend, spend an afternoon in nature, or simply treat yourself to a special moment.

839. Promotion

Your soul deserves attention.

Your angels want you to embrace your value as a contributor in your world. They want to honor you with a better position to do this. Take time today to review and revise your resume, reflect upon what you want in a career, or simply visualize what the next step can look like for you.

840. New Lessons

Truth is revealed.

You have leveled up your spiritual journey. Your angels acknowledge that what has been revealed to you is going to change your perspective from now on. Journal about how a recent truth has affected you and how you plan to accommodate its presence in your life from now on.

841. Regenerate

Infinite change is upon you!

The changes coming your way are a result of your past prayers and goals. The world will look different when you get what you want. How can you renew yourself to meet this new world? Clear your energy by diffusing essential oils, burning a white candle, and listening to some spiritual music.

842. Deliberate Sequences

The choices you make follow you.

How you do one thing, you do everything. Pay attention to your patterns today. Daily life rituals in the microcosm create the blueprint for the macrocosm. Make one routine you carry out today more of a ritual. With each step along the way, know you are creating the future.

843. Access Thoughts

Clear pathways to your soul.

When you open yourself up to new ideas, pathways form in which abundance flows. Your angels encourage you to read up on new ideas, partake in a community event, or simply try out some new music. Anything new today is what you are being called to pursue!

844. Safe

Feel secure in the divine.

Your angels want you to feel secure and safe in their watchful presence. You've been given an abundance of blessings recently. See these blessings and count them. As you do, lift a prayer to the angels for gifting them to you. No blessing is too small to count.

845. Level Up
Give yourself credit.

The new plans you create must honor the growth you've undergone. Spend time reflecting and reviewing past intentions, and note how they've come to pass. Reword the ones that have not, and add new ones reflective of additional growth you are ready to take on.

846. Appreciate Yourself
You already did it!

Your angels are asking you to notice that you've already done something big in your life. A huge goal that used to lie heavily on your mind has been achieved. Acknowledge it. Then, sit in awe and gratitude of what your dedication has produced.

847. Cluttered Path
Address procrastination.

When you deal with all the things you've let accumulate in your life, new pathways to abundance are created. Think of a present area of your life that has been on your mind recently. Take action to get it in order today.

848. Spiritual Development
Sense your power.

You are creating a bond with the divine. Your angels are sending you an abundance of messages, and your spiritual development will strengthen that connection. Lie in meditation and tap your third eye chakra (the center of the forehead) with your index finger. Repeat this mantra: "I see."

849. Spiritual Practices

Include the divine.

The choices coming your way need something added to them: They need a place in which to insert the role of the divine. Your angels would like you to contemplate how spiritual practices can become habitual.

850. Welcome Love

Love lives in you!

The divine source freely and consistently gives love to you. It lives within you always. Your angels want you to connect to this source energy and feel it radiating out through your being. Lie in meditation with your hands on your heart chakra. Repeat this mantra: "I welcome love."

851. Limitless Energy

Think outside the box.

The energy you are being fed is limitless! Your angels ask you to tap in to it today to get started on attaining a life goal. Brainstorm a list of ways you can get life moving in your favor. Don't hold back!

852. Overwhelm

Ask for clarity.

There are many choices coming at you at once, and your angels acknowledge the overwhelm that can come with choosing what's correct for you. They ask you to write down your thoughts today, sleep on them, and review them tomorrow. Clarity will come.

853. Congratulations

Self-discipline pays off.

Do you feel the pats on the back from your angels? They are congratulating you on your hard work, effort, and personal self-discipline. They know it wasn't easy, and they spotlight your willingness to live your best life. Do something celebratory for yourself today.

854. Perspective Change

Consider more opportunities.

This is a reminder that the more you put out there, the more you can fail—but also the more you can succeed! Your angels remind you that it is all about how you look at it. Today, think of a present situation and reflect on a different perspective from which you can view it.

855. Love Abundantly

Donate your time.

The love you have in your heart can be shared with those around you. Where can you demonstrate love to someone who doesn't feel any? Your guides want you to donate some time today to a person or an organization that would benefit from the abundance of love you have in your heart.

856. Domino Effect

Celebrate abundant joys!

As one wondrous thing happens in your life, so, too, will others! The abundance you have manifested and attracted is creating a domino effect. See where it takes place and celebrate this moment. Do something fun today, and really feel the joy channel through you.

857. Creative Flow

You are ready.

The creative flow of ideas is coming fast now. There is a lot being fed to you, and it's not essential you remember or absorb it all right now. In meditation, write down anything that comes up. Continue to write things down throughout the day.

858. Restoration

Receive love.

Love is coming your way! If you are single, get ready to meet new people. If you are in a relationship, be prepared for a wave of renewal. There is love in the air, and it always starts with you. Place your hands on your heart chakra and repeat this mantra: "I receive love."

859. Perfection

Embrace self-improvement.

Perfection is not the end goal: Self-improvement is. Your angels want you to know that the mistakes of the past were valuable contributors to the wonderful person you are today. Write about an error that taught you something, focusing on how the lessons of yesterday create a foundation for where you are today.

860. Self-Sufficiency

Giving is the reward.

Giving to others without any expectation of what you'll get back is a key element to prosperity in your life. There is so much love you have to give, and your angels encourage you to spread it around to those in need. Donate your time to a place or person who could use a little bit of extra love.

861. Making Concessions

Reflect on where you give in often.

It's okay for you to meet some people in the middle. Others, those who always have to be right, need to be weeded out. Think of who you are constantly giving in to: Your angels are alerting you that this is not a healthy relationship.

862. Snowball Effect

Don't put limits on abundance.

When one good thing happens, many more come with it! Your angels want you to embrace all the wonderful things coming your way. You do not have to put limits on your abundance: You are worth all of it. Repeat this mantra: "I am worthy and deserving."

863. Give Praise

Tell others how well they do.

Your angels tell you that when you notice the work people around you do, it not only makes them feel good; it also makes you feel good. Give someone the praise they deserve today; see how it creates warmth and joy to do so.

864. Nurture Blessings

Take a moment today!

There are so many blessings in your life presently. Your angels want you to notice one, feel immense gratitude for it, and spend time nurturing it today. This could be a relationship, a pet, or even a space that you call yours. Feel the divine energy exchanged as you do this.

865. Yearning
Explore self.

Today you are being asked to tap in to a primal force within you— the one that is constantly asking to discover, to learn, and to step out of the zone of comfort. Tap in to your desire. Pick up a new book, join a class with like-minded people, or try a new activity you've been thinking about.

866. Intent Matters
Look for the good.

When you get in the habit of looking for the good in others, you will let go of your need to judge them. See people in a compassionate light. Reflect on people in your life and their intentions toward you, rather than on their actions.

867. Cultivate Joy
Find joy in the moment.

Your angels ask you to embrace the challenge of finding joy today, in this very moment. Walk outside barefoot, sit in the sun, hear the birds chirp, and align yourself with the divine in order to feel pure and simple joy wash over you.

868. Absolve
Return the suffering.

You are being asked to free up some space in your spiritual body today by letting go of resentment toward someone who has hurt you. Sit in silence today, and envision the person you need to forgive. Give them back any suffering they inflicted upon you, and know that on some level, they receive it.

869. Wonder

Instead of worrying about it, wonder about it!

Instead of focusing on worrying about things you cannot control, wonder about them. Your angels ask you to change how you contemplate what is to come. Today, when faced with something that makes you think "I worry…" rephrase it in your self-talk to "I wonder…"

870. Unearth Knowledge

You have an innate ability.

You are being called to improve upon your existing connection to the divine. Your angels want you to learn more about connecting to yourself and spirit. Pick up a spiritual book, start a new podcast, or meet up with some like-minded people to get a group discussion flowing.

871. Restore Spirit

Lend your heart!

There is a person near you who needs support in some way. Listening to someone's problems, lending a hand to someone who needs a break, or helping someone get back up after a big failure is restorative not only to their spirit but to yours as well.

872. Learning Opportunity

Serve your highest self.

You are being presented with some big challenges, and your angels want you to reframe them as a significant moment in your life in which the best choice will serve your highest self. Take time today to contemplate your responses, and ask your angels for support.

873. Plentiful

Feel gratitude!

At this very moment, look around you. You are being called to see all that you have, all that is a result of your hard work and accomplishments, with a filter of gratitude. Lie in meditation with your hands on your root chakra (the base of the spine) and repeat this mantra: "I have plenty."

874. Affirm Yourself

Repeat positive things often.

Affirmations are essential for you to get through the present time. Your angels want you to double down on your recitation of affirmations throughout your day. Repeat them often during mundane tasks, such as brushing your teeth, driving, or showering.

875. One Step

Avoid overwhelm.

One thing at a time is the message from your angels today. They are signaling that when it comes to changing an aspect of your life, you are taking on too much at once. Today, choose just one goal and stick with it for thirty days. Track your progress!

876. Alone

Not everyone will get it.

The more aligned to your higher self you are—the more connected to spirit you feel—the more isolation you can experience from people around you. Think about how quality is more important than quantity, and create a plan for a fun outing with a like-minded friend.

877. Learn More

Where are your fears coming from?

Your fears are indicative of something much larger and more subconscious within you. Today, spend some time digging behind your fears, into what caused them in the first place. Journal, talk to a professional, or contemplate in nature.

878. Abundant Language

Speak well of yourself!

How you speak to yourself matters, and your angels are asking you to observe your self-talk more closely. The words you use when speaking to yourself and of yourself are creating your reality. Take the role of observer today in all your thoughts and words. See what you notice.

879. Tap In

Receive wisdom.

Your intuition needs development, as your angels are sending you spiritual downloads now more than ever. Prioritize your connection to the divine. Lie in meditation with your hands on your crown chakra (the top of the head). Repeat this mantra: "I receive wisdom."

880. Acknowledge Signs

Choose a symbol.

Ask for your angels' communication. You are being told to choose a sign that resonates with you specifically. Choose a number, animal, or other symbol that resonates with you and receive the message when you see it appearing in your life.

881. Use It

First impressions are important!

You are downloading spiritual information and messages at an increased rate lately. Your angels invite you to trust it and begin using it. Feel confident in what your first impressions are of a person or situation in your life. Write down what you feel for future reference.

882. No Obstructions

Embrace silence today.

Limit distractions as spiritual messages, inspirations, and images flood into your thoughts and feelings. You are being asked to stay aware of your angels' messages by steering clear of the things that can drown out their calls to you. Sit in silence for ten minutes today.

883. Your Worth

The material world is temporary.

The way to be free is to untie yourself from material possessions. Your angels are asking you to focus on the intangible abundance around you rather than on the tangible things you have. Write down ten intrinsic lessons you've learned that you hold dear.

884. Self-Realization

You've found your true path!

You are being applauded by your angels! The realizations you have had recently are a breakthrough. Your life has pivoted onto the course of your soul's plan. Take time today to celebrate this. Spend time in nature feeling the gratitude for the path that brought you self-realization.

885. Your Lens

Choose your own perspective.

There is a difference between what feels right for you and what feels right for others. Right now your angels have you facing a choice that will make that even clearer. Go forth and choose your own perspective instead of the perspectives of those around you.

886. Identity

You are your own person!

Your angels are proud of you for securing your own identity amid the strong personalities around you who often want you to take on their causes instead of your own. Celebrate yourself today by writing a letter describing all the things about you that you love.

887. In Alignment

Reward yourself!

Choices you've recently made have put you in better alignment with your desires and goals. You are being applauded for your hard-won victories. Take a moment today and reward yourself with inner peace, a long bath, a walk in nature, or a self-care practice of your choosing.

888. Good Job

Make space for more.

You are doing well, and your angels are proud of you. Take a look around and practice gratitude for how far you've come. Abundance in some form is coming to you now. Make space in your life to allow the universe to take things into its own hands. List the fears you have and release them.

889. Broaden Yourself

Impart your wisdom.

The work you have done in self-reflection has led to amazing personal growth. Your angels are proud of your ability to take your traumas and transmute them into healing wisdom. Find a context in which another person could use the hard-won advice and support you have to give.

890. Higher-Self Closure

Let it all go now.

You don't need to have an actual conversation with someone in order to have closure with them. Your angels encourage you to visualize the higher self of the person or situation you want to let go. Speak your thoughts to their higher self and know that on some level, it was received.

891. Create Emphasis

Avoid distractions.

The abundance of spiritual downloads you've been experiencing is wonderful, but can also lead to overwhelm and distraction. Do one thing at a time. Write down everything you get done, but choose one goal to stick with today until it's completed.

892. Accept Love

Say yes to support.

There are many people who want to reach out to you. Allow those who love you to help you. Practice saying yes today to those who reach out with support, love, and guidance. Let yourself be nurtured by the people who care.

893. Trusted Universe

Step into the unknown.

The universe has an abundance of opportunity for you, but you have to step into the unknown to receive it. Your angels support you and remind you to not let fear hold you back from growth. Repeat this mantra: "I trust the universe."

894. Move Forward

Keep on going.

Focusing on moving forward is the message delivered by your angels today. You are encouraged to put blinders on to outside distractions that make giving up look like your best option. Repeat this mantra: "I am capable of great things."

895. Ask Yourself

Question your beliefs.

Your angels want you to explore the subconscious thoughts that hold you back. These are self-limiting beliefs! Reflect on long-held thoughts such as not being creative or not being good at speaking to a group. Then make a plan to challenge them.

896. Be Faithful

Live an authentic life.

Be real about what you know to be true about yourself. Your angels advise you against putting yourself in situations you aren't prepared for or passionate about. Own your truth and see where you can limit exposure to things that don't reflect it.

897. Advocate

Be the voice!

The opportunities you've had in life are here not just for your own gain but for others as well. Today, think of a way you can advocate for someone. Lift another up by calling attention to their cause, creating a space for them to shine, or giving them a leg up where they would not otherwise have one.

898. Share Love

Treat yourself and another.

Your angels suggest that what you do for yourself today you do for another. Think of someone else and treat them to something you were about to treat yourself to. Feel their appreciation and love as you share the experience.

899. Gather Information

Research the future.

The more you research and incorporate knowledge from the future, the more aligned you become with that reality. Take the time today to gather information and resources you need for the changes you wish to come. Enjoy the process and feel the higher vibrations reaching you.

900. Effects

What you give, you get.

All that you have put out there has been collected and multiplied and is ready to be sent back to you. What realizations have you had in recent interactions with people and places? Write about a lesson you've learned and how you plan to use it to grow.

901. Turning Page

Now is your time to begin again.

A chapter has closed in your life. Reinventing yourself is not easy, but it is necessary. Embracing the reality and combining it with the confidence that you are ready to move ahead is your angels' message now. Repeat this mantra: "I will know what to do when faced with something new."

902. Embrace Setbacks

Failure is an opportunity.

The so-called failures of the past are not meant to be dwelled upon in negativity; instead they are meant for you to learn from so as to make better choices today. Write about a mistake you've made and how it contributed to your overall personal growth.

903. Navigate

Look at your game plan.

The present situation can be tricky to navigate, but your angels applaud your efforts. Your determination and stamina are not unnoticed by the divine. Take a step back today and reconsider your game plan for moving forward. Fortify yourself where you can and eliminate what no longer serves you.

904. Life Purpose

Your values hold the key to your life's purpose.

Your angels ask you to look inward to your core beliefs and take from there what your next steps need to be. Write down your core values, and reflect on what life would look like if you were living in alignment with them.

905. Free Flowing

Be wondrous.

Following the flow is your message today. Get into such a state of wondrous thought that you don't notice the time or the world going on around you. Start a creative pursuit, spend a day in nature, or get into that book you've been wanting to read. Let it carry you away.

906. Materials Balanced

Life is a balancing act.

Your angels remind you to care more for the spiritual connection you carry than for the connection you have to the material world. It's a never-ending balancing act, but your angels are supporting you through it. Repeat this mantra: "I connect to the divine!"

907. Shift Struggle

Move the energy along.

Hard work is inevitable and will come when you are doing something worthwhile. Struggle is when you are stuck in one spot and cannot seem to move forward. Look to where you feel there is struggle in your life and brainstorm ways to move that energy along.

908. Spiritual Space

Create time and space for your growth!

You are being called to create space for your spiritual growth. Your angels are asking you to develop new habits of mind in which to foster an abundance mindset. Today, carve out time and space to do just that.

909. Embrace Today

You are confident.

Starting over will mean new experiences, adventures, and mistakes. Get in a mindset where you can embrace all of this as part of a better whole. Lie in meditation with your hands on your root chakra (the base of the spine). Repeat this mantra: "I am confident in my abilities."

910. Speak Wisely

Words affect everything.

Your words have power, so it's important to stay cognizant of them. How you speak about yourself is how the universe will view you. As you start new chapters, you need to reintroduce new positive mantras. Today, create a mantra for yourself you can use to elevate the vibration of your life.

911. Lightworker

You are being called upon.

Your guides call upon you to use your spiritual development to inspire others. Seeing this number is a message that you possess the gifts of spirit to remind people that their higher power rests inside them. The time is now to make changes in your life work so as to carry out this divine calling!

912. New Beginnings

The future is now.

You've worked too hard not to take this final step toward your future. The road ahead is less traveled, but it's your road. You will make your own way now. But you are never alone: Your angels are with you. Write down a fear you have about the unknown, then burn or bury the paper as a symbol of your newfound freedom.

913. Career Growth

Invest in yourself.

New career opportunities are coming through. But you'll have to invest in your professional growth to take the next steps. What is a skill you've been putting off mastering? Today, take a step to get it done.

914. Equality

It takes two.

Is there a pattern of inequality in listening, giving, and supporting in your relationships? Your angels call on you to notice it and self-advocate. Where can you give more in a current relationship? Where can you receive more? Repeat this mantra: "I communicate my needs."

915. Prosperity

When you have more, you give more.

Prosperity is coming to you because your angels know you will be in a better position to help others when you yourself are secure and comfortable. Make a small donation to an organization you hold dear. Consider making it in the amount reflective of this angel number!

916. End Point

A chapter in love has closed.

Love is never lost, but it does change forms. Your angels support you and send unconditional love your way. Spend time in nature today to ground yourself. Take a walk in the grass barefoot, swim in a body of water, or simply lie in the sun as you process the next steps to take.

917. Sudden Shifts

Life happens in a moment.

Your angels signal to you that your current reality is shifting toward something very different. It's all for your highest good, but change can cause anxiety and stress. Let go of the fear of what is to come. As you sit in meditation today, breathe in the white light of faith and breathe out the darker light of fear.

918. Freedom

Choose you!

Self-reliance is your ticket to freedom. You are being called to make choices that reflect that. Recognize the current patterns of your life and contemplate how you can create new patterns that reflect self-sufficiency.

919. Routine

Notice the things you do without thinking.

Your angels call upon you today to drop a bad habit and replace it with a good one. Negative self-talk is a habit they especially want you to focus on. List a few habits you've been meaning to tackle and make a step toward one of them today.

920. Amity

Create peace in your relationships.

Ongoing conflicts and issues need your attention. It's time to end anything that is not in your control. Moving forward and moving on is what your angels are urging you to do. Revamp a family tradition today. Bake a favorite recipe or re-create a cherished memory with the ones you love.

921. Hello, You

You are becoming exactly who you always were!

As things fall away and change presents itself, your angels remind you that this is another step toward becoming exactly who you already always were. Repeat this mantra: "I love who I am becoming."

922. Begin Again

Set new intentions.

You are being called to create new intentions to manifest. Today, reflect thoroughly in a journal on what you have already received. Feel gratitude as you do this. Then create a list of new intentions you are setting.

923. Self-Direct

You are your own compass.

There are people around you who have many suggestions for your life, but your angels remind you that only you know what's best for you. Sit down with a present conundrum in your life and create a plan of action that is entirely your own.

924. Farewell

Look fondly on what was.

Your angels acknowledge that you are letting go of things that once served you well, and they remind you that it's necessary to do so. Connect to them in gratitude as you let go. Repeat this mantra: "I am grateful for the life I live."

925. Challenge Yourself

Do something new and exciting!

The authentic you wants to explore this world, and your angels are encouraging this. What is an activity out your comfort zone that could make you feel more alive? Plan it today, either alone or with a friend who can add to your enthusiasm.

926. Spiritual Possessions

Material possessions are minuscule compared to spiritual blessings.

You are being called today to reflect on what you have and to bask in gratitude and awe of these things. Journal about your spiritual possessions, such as compassion, appreciation, empathy, and other gifts you've been given that make what you have in the material world enough.

927. Self-Secure

You've got this!

There are changes on the way, but you are asked to let go of any fear toward them. Lie in meditation with your hands over your solar plexus chakra (just above the navel). Repeat this mantra: "I am confident; I can do anything."

928. Sacred Space

Make your own spiritual place.

You need a place that is all your own to feel safe in. Create a sacred space today for your prayers, meditations, and self-care. A corner of a room, a bathroom, or a little garden will work just fine. Make it your own.

929. Spiritual Instincts

Establish your soul relationship.

Your abilities to connect with the divine are being strengthened. Through this number, your angels call upon you to trust this fact and connect to them. Lie with your hands on your crown chakra (the top of the head). Repeat this mantra: "I am connected."

930. Expand

Life reflects the work you put into it.

The work you've put in, the prayers you've sent, the sacrifices you've made—they create a new reality. But that reality will look different, and it can be frightening. Your angels remind you of this as they send you a message to always be receptive to growth. Journal about what that means to you.

931. Sincerity

Feel joyous for others!

When you sincerely want something for others, the rewards they reap will be yours as well. The way to multiply your own blessings is by truly feeling joy for the ones others have received. Think of a person in your life and list the reasons why you are happy for them.

932. Rash Decisions

Sleep on it.

There is a situation in your life that does not need your immediate emotional response. No matter how urgent it may feel, your angels encourage you against making a choice today. Take some time to process your options, and give yourself a calm timeline to make a wise decision.

933. Soul-Searching

It has always been within you.

The world around you will change, but you have a peaceful eternal connection within you always. Lie in meditation with your hands over your heart chakra. Repeat this mantra: "I am the universe."

934. Energy Analysis

How do you affect others?

It is time to gather up all your self-awareness and reflect on how you affect others. Contemplate yourself in all contexts of your life (friendships, coworkers, family, and self), and review how your energy radiates out and in what manner.

935. Embrace Yourself

The new version of you needs love too.

Your angels call you to check in on yourself. The things you've been going through need attention. Lie in meditation with your hands on your heart chakra. Repeat this mantra: "I accept myself."

936. Help Another

Your struggles today allow you to heal others tomorrow.

The work you have done—the struggles you've overcome—is not for nothing. Struggle exists so you can assist others in their own, similar challenges. You are being called to consider how to practice lightwork (spiritual work in service to others). Journal about how you could uniquely help people who are at stages of life you've left behind.

937. Hold Yourself

Your health is precious.

The person you tend to ignore the most is yourself. Your angels want you to focus time on your health today. Make that appointment you've been putting off or start a health regimen you know you need. What can you do today to show yourself that you value your health?

938. Determination

You'll get through this.

You work hard for the things you appreciate the most. The doors will open for you, but when they do, there will be hard work behind them. Repeat this mantra: "I am powerful; I can do anything I set my mind to!"

939. Details Matter

Be meticulous.

The present situation you are in could use some attention to details. Tie up loose ends, make the calls that you've been procrastinating, and establish a plan to get stalled projects completed. Don't waste any time getting to that today.

940. Flexibility

Your strength lies in your ability to accept what is.

The only thing that will ever be consistent is change. Your angels are reminding you that your adaptability is a key goal to have in mind right now. Make a list of what you can currently control and what you cannot.

941. Reap Rewards

Thank yourself!

A project you've been working on is coming to an end. With that comes relief but also a feeling of "what's next?" Today, simply bask in the joy of completion. List the ways you forged ahead when you were unsure you could. Thank yourself for your own resolve.

942. Finalized

Finish what you started.

The moment you made a choice long ago created a stream of events that is coming to a conclusion soon. Write thoughtfully about the effects this choice has had in your life, and note the differences in yourself between the start of this and now, as you near the finish.

943. New Timeline

Reenergize yourself.

As you find yourself at the end of one timeline, another one has already begun. It's time to reenergize yourself and create new goals and dreams to manifest. Spend a good amount of time in nature today; feel the earth and sun ground you, clearing new pathways for intentions to flow.

944. Advise

You are called to lightwork!

You are being called to give counsel to those around you in need of it. Your angels urge you to lightwork (spiritual work in service to others) to remind others where the divine lives in them. Several times today repeat this mantra: "I am lightness; I radiate peace to others."

945. Feel Love

Angels will not leave your side.

Today, simply feel the love the universe has for you. Bask in the glow of feeling supported and protected. Know that the things that come your way are negative or positive based on your own perspective. Lie in meditation and feel the divine light connect to your heart chakra.

946. Your Spark

Follow your curiosity.

It is time to refocus your calling! What is a new path you feel drawn to? A whole new chapter is starting for you, but you have to be willing to follow it. Follow your curiosity today in anything you so choose. See what it sparks inside you.

947. Eliminating Stagnancy

Feel proud of yourself.

Your recent efforts to clear up stagnant areas in your life are being applauded by your angels. They want you to sit in the present moment and feel all the benefits of the work you've done. Sit in nature today and let yourself feel glad and proud of your accomplishments.

948. Revisit Intentions

Out with the old!

This is a call to reflect and revisit some old intentions. Your angels show you that you've already attained some of them, and others need to be reworked. Spend time today reading past intentions and journaling about new ones that reflect your soul growth.

949. Be Fluid

Make a graceful transition.

As you go from one set of goals to a new set, your angels ask you to be fluid in your transition. Contemplate who you need to thank, look to where you still need closure, and journal about your life lessons.

950. Heart Truths

Love from a distance.

The love you have for others can be demonstrated in a multitude of ways. The people in your life who cannot be trusted to reciprocate can be loved from a distance. Visualize the higher self of an individual you struggle to love sitting with you today. Speak your truth to them from the heart.

951. Take Pause

Stop, look around, and reflect.

Your angels are feeding you information today about what direction to go next. Your energy is abundant, and they want you to make sure you're putting it toward a worthwhile cause. Take a break today. Sit in solace and ask for clarity.

952. New Level

Endings are beginnings.

You've mastered a skill you've been working on for a long time. Now it's time to refocus and choose another one. Get inspired today as you focus on research and think about what is next!

953. Fortitude

What you did takes bravery.

Your angels see your struggles and support you in your efforts. They admire your willingness to do what's right in the present circumstances even when others don't always agree. Receive their praise while lying in meditation today.

954. Finish Line

Honor learning opportunities.

The completion of one area of your life is coming up, and your angels want you to celebrate the lessons learned. Today, create a list of what you have learned about yourself and how these things tie into you moving forward to the next phase of life.

955. Romantic Relationships

Reconfigure the connections!

You are being asked to change up your way of doing things in romance. Whether you are single or in a relationship, your angels would like you to take today to reflect and reconfigure how you go about connecting with others.

956. Slow Down

You earned it.

The hard work you've put in has not gone unnoticed by your angels. In fact, they were beside you the whole time, working in their high-vibrational realm to support you. Today, take a nap or a salt bath, or just be at peace and solace at your leisure. Feel the peace fall upon you.

957. Go Forth

Stick with your decisions.

The choice you made is one you need to stick with. Your angels guard against vacillating any further: It is just delaying the bigger picture. Lie in meditation today with your hands on your solar plexus chakra (just above the navel) and repeat this mantra: "I am confident."

958. Plateau

Be in the moment.

Perhaps you've been feeling stagnant, as if you've been walking along an endless plateau. Your angels are signaling that this is over. They ask you to be in the moment today because there are things coming your way that will need your mindful attention.

959. Valuable Insight

Take pride in hard-won truths.

There is no way you could have learned what you know today if not for the unique challenges you've been through. Your angels want you to value your insight because it was hard-won and rightly earned. Write about a lesson learned from experience, and how you use it to this day.

960. Admit

When you are wrong, own it.

Your angels are signaling that you need to take some time today to recognize how you act when you make a mistake. When have you done something and not taken full accountability for it? Contemplate this, and realize that acknowledgment is the biggest step there is.

961. End Conflict

Be assertive today.

You are being reminded that you can choose to end an unpleasant conflict simply by disengaging from it. Your angels are pointing to a situation in which you feel the need to constantly defend yourself. Reflect on how you can assertively let the other party know that you will no longer be participating in this discussion!

962. Life Values

Reflect on reinforced beliefs.

What you have gone through has fortified core values as well as allowed you to see things differently. Your angels know you had to rethink some things that you once thought were true. But they want you to focus on the values that have been reinforced. Write about one of those today.

963. Expectations

Release the control.

What you want will come to you, but it will be in divine timing and form. Your angels want you to manage your expectations for what things will look like when they arrive. Write what you want and release it into the universe today, knowing it will come to you when and how it's ready.

964. Prayers Answered

Intentions have been realized!

An intention you set out into the universe a long time ago has been realized. Your angels want you to take the time today to notice this, to acknowledge it, and to spend focused time appreciating it. Write about how your life has been blessed with prayers answered.

965. Live Differently

Switch up your patterns.

The ways you speak, the habits you form, and your mindless daily routines are all under a microscope. Your angels want you to do things differently. The little changes you make that create discomfort in the short term will become life-changing in the long run.

966. Complaining

Shift your focus.

Your angels alert you to monitoring your interior and exterior dialogue. They want you to notice where you've been complaining and shift your focus. Instead of seeing the lack in your life, look for the opportunity to learn a lesson. Repeat this mantra: "I see the good."

967. Inner Critic

Confront the ego.

The voice inside your head that critiques and judges you is not from the divine. It's your own ego beating you down. Your angels want you to confront your inner critic today by being mindful of the thoughts that come your way. Ask yourself, "Is this necessary, productive, or kind?"

968. Relax

Feel loved.

There is a need at times to simply absorb what you've been through, the lessons you've learned, and the love you have for self and spirit. Today is the day to do just that. Sit with your favorite music or in the sounds of nature, or simply be silent and feel the overwhelming love that is abundantly available to you.

969. Fear

Excitement lies ahead!

Instead of seeing the worst that can happen in the present situation, contemplate the excitement in it. Turning your perspective from fear to excitement is a tool your angels want you to use today. List things that you are fearful of and try to creatively turn them into things you can get excited about.

970. Spirit Place

Your spiritual sanctuary is necessary.

You need a space of your own to connect with the divine. Your angels are asking you to make your spiritual comfort a priority. Set up a corner of a room or a special spot in the garden, or make the bathroom a sanctuary.

971. Promote Tranquility

Your voice matters.

There is a situation around you that you could help or hinder by adding your own viewpoints. Your angels encourage you to come to this moment with a vision of promoting peace and wellness for all parties. Today, use your voice to help others see the peaceful solutions!

972. No Drama

You embody peace.

You may be finding that you don't care anymore about the cyclical drama of those around you. It doesn't make you feel alive; in fact, you prefer lately to live without it. Finding peace has been life-changing for you. Your angels applaud you. Repeat this mantra: "I embody peace."

973. Take Action

Do away with procrastination!

The thing you've been procrastinating about ends today. You are being called to take action and move this along. Make a plan of what to do and start with the first step. Stick to your plan.

974. Forgo Multitasking

Take it one thing at a time.

Instead of multitasking, your angels suggest that you finish just one thing at a time. Take the task at hand that is most pressing, and focus all your energy only there. When done, then you can transition to the next task.

975. Reward Growth

Be proud of how far you have come.

Every little accomplishment needs acknowledgment. Your personal growth is being applauded by your angels, and they want you to join in. Treat yourself today to some special self-care. Relish your personal growth and feel proud!

976. Detachment

Contemplate spiritual shifts.

Detachment from drama and things that are of no value to you anymore is a sign of a spiritual shift. Where once you partook in drama or in scenarios that wasted your energy, you don't have an urge to do so anymore. Reflect on this today.

977. Rewire Yourself
Use your brain differently.

The fear and anxiety you experience will be lessened if you start using your brain differently. The practices of yoga, physical activity, and meditation over time rewire our thinking. Try something today to give yourself a break from the usual anxiety.

978. Pay Attention
Notice your strengths.

Your strengths are asking to be noticed. The things you are good at, you tend to dismiss as unimportant. Shift your thinking today; notice what you are doing well at and where others respond to you successfully. Nothing is too little to acknowledge!

979. Aim Ahead
Learn about yourself.

Your angels are signaling that your vivid dreams—both daydreams and those had when sleeping at night—are tools for you to learn more about yourself. Journal today about which themes seem to be constant in your mind's wanderings. Symbols are important.

980. Inspiration
Follow a passion.

You are being asked to get inspired in life. The next chapter is awaiting you, but you need to engage your passion to receive it. Pick up a new book that interests you, begin a creative pursuit, or make a plan to do something you've been wanting to do.

981. Accept Knowledge
You can't go back.

Your angels acknowledge that now that you know what you know, your life has forever changed. Take time today to acknowledge the information you presently have and compare it to where you were before. Make peace with the changes that will be forthcoming.

982. In Sync

Ideas flow when you feel good!

Creating a healthy routine of physical, mental, and spiritual practices will allow for new ideas and angel messages to flow in. Make some time today for a walk, meditation, and a healthy meal. Feel yourself respond to your self-love.

983. You Decide

Go in your own direction.

In all things, make sure you are the one deciding which direction to go in. Your angels are encouraging you to have confidence in your ability to make good choices for yourself. Consider a choice you have to make and take time to contemplate why you are making it.

984. Self-Care

Love yourself.

Increasing your self-care instead of your expectations is what you are being called to do today. Instead of waiting for someone to do something you wish they would do, do it for yourself! Create a reality in which you don't need others to make you feel good—you can do that yourself!

985. Bliss

Live in the present moment.

The joy of being in this moment far outweighs what you have been chasing after for so long. Your angels want to let you in on a secret: The way to be happy is to live in the here and now. Spend time today enjoying the present moment. When your mind wanders, bring it back.

986. Forthright

Practice saying no.

Your angels are asking you to stop confusing yes with no. They alert you that people know you have a hard time not doing what they ask you to, and they have been taking advantage. Practice saying no in the mirror ten times today.

987. Introspection

Get honest with yourself.

Introspection is necessary at this time. Your angels are saying that before moving forward, a debriefing of the soul is needed. Take careful inventory of what your motivations are and check them against what you know your authentic life looks like.

988. Positive Habits

New chances for expansion surround you.

You are being called to build upon your positive habits. In every situation, there is opportunity to learn, grow, and challenge yourself. Your angels are encouraging you to develop a habit of mind to approach any situation in this way. Write about where you can do this today.

989. Devotion

Heal others.

The work you've done within is now bringing you down a new path. Your angels are encouraging you to devote your life to imparting wisdom and healing to others. You are being called to do healing work. Think about how this plays a role in your goals and dreams.

990. Mastery

Closure is yours!

Take your control back today in regard to a present situation that is over and done with. Your angels remind you that you are the master of your own reactions. Let go of what someone else thinks of you, practice self-validation, or write a letter to someone you need to end an unhealthy relationship with.

991. Words

Speak what you want into existence.

Your words are magical: They carry the highest vibrations toward you. You are being asked to use them. When conversing with a friend today, speak with excitement and joy about what you are setting out to achieve.

992. Express Yourself

Form your reaction.

Expressing your reaction to what's happening around you is welcomed by your angels. They want you to form your own response in a productive way. Write in your journal, draw something representative of your emotional state, or have a meaningful conversation with a friend who is understanding.

993. Soul Groups

Take good advice!

As one door closes and another opens, you are encouraged to reach out to people who have been through this before. Connect with friends or an online support group and practice introducing yourself to new people who can show you the way.

994. Honor Goals

Examine your current opportunities.

You are being redirected to make decisions that honor your goals rather than your short-term gratification. The opportunities presented to you currently need careful examination. Ask yourself if they will help you or hold you back from your ultimate dreams and goals.

995. Keep Exploring

Create new goals.

All your relationships, current opportunities, and living situations can be explored. You are being urged to level up your expectations by deep-diving and seeing how to improve each facet of your life. Write down some goals you have for the different areas of your life.

996. Self-Examine

Live authentically.

Now that you understand yourself better, you have to make choices that reflect this truth. The life you used to lead is no more; you are ready for what is next! Journal about what transitions your life needs to make so as to accommodate this new self-awareness.

997. Initiate Change

Lead others to helping a cause.

You are being called to lead others in giving back. Your angels surround you with support and guidance as you consider what you are going to do to unite others in helping a cause. Begin researching and create a game plan for how you can get to work on this today.

998. Acknowledgment

Receive with grace!

You are being gifted something quite special, and your angels encourage you to receive it willingly with love and gratitude. Simply take what you are given and say thank you, not only to them but to the universe as well.

999. Fulfillment

Visualize what's next.

The cycle of what you have been doing is reaching fulfillment. You are at the finish line of your goals, and it's time to start leveling up to visualize some new ones. What can you do to tie up loose ends? Explore this question today.

Part 3

ANGEL
NUMBERS LOG

The relationship with your angels is fortified when you pay attention to the messages they send. Angel numbers are nudges meant to put you on your authentic path—the one your soul desires to journey upon. Recording these numbers, along with where and when you saw them, and how you felt when you saw them, will not only enhance your ability to decipher angel numbers, but will also heighten your own intuition and alertness to the spiritual world around you. By writing down what you see, you are setting forth a distinct path. You are decreeing to the universe itself that you are willing and open to the messages it brings you, and are ready to become the best version of yourself and create a reality that best suits your soul's purpose. Your angels stand beside you, supporting you all the way.

ANGEL NUMBER:

Where You Saw It:	
When You Saw It:	
Your Emotional State at the Time of Its Appearance:	
Codex Definition:	

Reflection:

_____

_____

_____

_____

_____

_____

_____

_____

ANGEL NUMBER:

Where You Saw It:	
When You Saw It:	
Your Emotional State at the Time of Its Appearance:	
Codex Definition:	

Reflection:

_____

_____

_____

_____

_____

_____

_____

ANGEL NUMBER:

Where You Saw It:	
When You Saw It:	
Your Emotional State at the Time of Its Appearance:	
Codex Definition:	

Reflection:

_____

_____

_____

_____

_____

_____

_____

_____

ANGEL NUMBER:

Where You Saw It:	
When You Saw It:	
Your Emotional State at the Time of Its Appearance:	
Codex Definition:	

Reflection:

ANGEL NUMBER:

Where You Saw It:	
When You Saw It:	
Your Emotional State at the Time of Its Appearance:	
Codex Definition:	

Reflection:

_____

_____

_____

_____

_____

_____

_____

ANGEL NUMBER:

Where You Saw It:	
When You Saw It:	
Your Emotional State at the Time of Its Appearance:	
Codex Definition:	

Reflection:

ANGEL NUMBER:

Where You Saw It:	
When You Saw It:	
Your Emotional State at the Time of Its Appearance:	
Codex Definition:	

Reflection:

_____

_____

_____

_____

_____

_____

_____

ANGEL NUMBER:

Where You Saw It:	
When You Saw It:	
Your Emotional State at the Time of Its Appearance:	
Codex Definition:	

Reflection:

ANGEL NUMBER:

Where You Saw It:	
When You Saw It:	
Your Emotional State at the Time of Its Appearance:	
Codex Definition:	

Reflection:

_____

_____

_____

_____

_____

_____

_____

_____

ANGEL NUMBER:

Where You Saw It:	
When You Saw It:	
Your Emotional State at the Time of Its Appearance:	
Codex Definition:	

Reflection: